Tchaiko

Simon Mundy

Other titles in the series

The Illustrated Lives of the Great Composers.

Tchaikovsky

Simon Mundy

OMNIBUS PRESS
London/New York/Sydney

For June

Cover design and art direction by Pearce Marchbank
Cover photography by Julian Hawkins
Text design by Hilite

Copyright © 1998 by Simon Mundy
This edition published in 1998 by Omnibus Press, a division of Book Sales Limited

ISBN 0.7119.6651.6
Order No.OP48021

Exclusive Distributors
Book Sales Limited,
8/9 Frith Street,
London W1V 5TZ, UK.

Music Sales Corporation,
257 Park Avenue South,
New York, NY 10010, USA.

Five Mile Press,
22 Summit Road, Noble Park,
Victoria 3174, Australia.

To the Music Trade only:
Music Sales Limited,
8/9, Frith Street,
London W1V 5TZ, UK.

Special thanks are due to Nikki Russell for her exhaustive picture research
and to Jo Shapcott for casting an eye over the manuscript.

Illustration credits:
Mary Evans Picture Library: 9,12,18,135,143,163;
Fotomas Index: 20,39,131,146,161,190;
Peter Joslin: 42,53,58,79,86,157,192b;
Lebrecht Collection: 10,14,17,26,29,34,40,45,46,50,54,56,59,60,62,70,71,
73,76,78,81,82,83,87,92,94,99,101,102,104,109,110,112,120,121,122,125,
133,136,141,144,147,150,152,154,156,160,162,164,165,168,170,171,172,
177,178,179,180,185,187,189,192t,193,195,197,199;
Novosti: 67,89,114,148,181,183,194;
Michael Reynolds Collection: 175.

Printed in the United Kingdom by Redwood Books, Trowbridge, Wiltshire.

A catalogue record for this book is available from the British Library.

Visit Omnibus Press at http://www.omnibuspress.com

Contents

Preface

The problem with writing a biography of Tchaikovsky over a century after his death is the sheer volume of information available, even in English sources. He was a man who did not believe in keeping quiet in writing, even if he was shy and modest in person. Not only did he write an astonishing number of letters, detailing almost everything in his professional and personal life, he kept an occasional diary which illuminates the emotional corners of his complex personality. To this has to be added the fact that a vast number of his friends and acquaintances remembered him in print. David Brown, the foremost Tchaikovsky scholar writing in English, complains that even in four volumes he had to compress and select more than he would have wished.

Despite this heap of documents Tchaikovsky remains an elusive character. Against the popular legend of an over-wrought, impossibly highly strung homosexual, pouring his unhappiness into works of unprecedented subjectivity, one has to balance a picture of another Tchaikovsky: the one his contemporaries saw more often. This man was a musician whose professionalism was greater than any composer in Russia until that time, a teacher who inspired great devotion and who gave his money and time generously to students and performers, a man who went to great lengths to mediate in family and business disputes, an inveterate (though often reluctant) traveller, excellent company into the small hours in the restaurants of Russia, France, Italy and Germany (all of whose languages he spoke with ease), and, as a composer-conductor, one of the first great international superstars. His sex life was active and not as clandestine as pursed-lipped biographers have wanted us to believe. Tchaikovsky was a man who gave and received love wherever he went. Of all the great composers he wrote music that was immediately popular and, if some of it is not of consistently high quality, enough is of transcending brilliance to ensure that he will remain one of the nineteenth century's most appealing figures. Many people reading this book will know the ballets, concertos and symphonies. Too much of his music is rarely heard, though, especially the songs, operas and chamber music. I hope the following pages will tempt people to explore.

Names and dates require decisions when writing about Russia in English. For names, I have generally picked the most familiar form even if scholarly opinion usually opts for something more accurate to phonetic transliteration (for example, Nicholai rather than Nikolay and Rachmaninov rather than Rakhmaninov). There are occasional exceptions. I prefer Evgeny Onegin to the rather less euphonious Eugene, for instance. Dates given are for the modern calendar, which is twelve days ahead of that operating in Russia in Tchaikovsky's lifetime. Some of the books in the bibliography opt for the original dates, some for both, but since so much of Tchaikovsky's life was spent travelling, the date used internationally seems the most convenient and the least confusing for today's readers.

Simon Mundy,
Gladestry, Radnor,
May, 1997.

Chapter 1

From Votkinsk to St Petersburg

Votkinsk lies on an insignificant tributary of the Volga a thousand miles in a straight line east of St Petersburg. If one went the same distance south-west of the Imperial Russian capital one would reach the Dutch border. Now Votkinsk can be reached by a railway branch line from Izhvetsk, linking it in one direction to Kazan and eventually Moscow, in the other to the old provincial centre of Viatka (renamed Kirov in the Soviet era) and the northern line to St Petersburg. In 1840, when Ilya Petrovich Tchaikovsky was Director of Mines in the town, there was not yet a railway to Votkinsk and the journey from St Petersburg by coach could take as much as three weeks. It was on the border of the last province before one came to the Ural mountains and the end of European Russia. Ilya Tchaikovsky had moved there three years before with his second wife, a French girl called Alexandra Assier. In 1840 he was 45, his wife was only 26 though they had already been married for seven years and had a son of two, Nicholai. In the household there was also eleven year-old Zinaida Illinishna, Ilya's daughter by his first marriage to Maria Keiser who had died soon after her birth.

The house in Votkinsk in which Pyotr Ilyich was born. The years of childhood spent here were the most stable and happiest of Tchaikovsky's life.

Being Director of Mines in Votkinsk made Ilya Tchaikovsky one of the most important government officials in the area, which depended on the mines and the iron works they supplied for the town's existence. As well as the industrial duties, the post gave him command of several serfs and a substantial force of Cossack guards. It was a considerable responsibility and one which carried with it social position and respect, though not the deference that would have come with aristocratic title or inherited estate. Neither did it carry with it the distinction of senior military service that his brothers Ivan and Pyotr had earned, Ivan giving his life fighting against Napoleon the year before Waterloo. Nonetheless Ilya's post demanded administrative competence and managerial ability and if it did not require the same level of intuitive imagination that a life in the arts would have done, nor did it mean that he was of only moderate intelligence, as so many of his son's biographers delight in suggesting. In fact Ilya Tchaikovsky's home was one where, in the drawing-room society of nineteenth-century Russia, his neighbours, many of them capable scientists, found warm hospitality and good conversation.

On 7 May 1840 (in the Western calendar – 25 April in the Russian calendar then still in use) Alexandra bore a second son. The proud parents named him after his grandfather and his distinguished and decorated soldier uncle, Pyotr. If they were hoping that he would enter the family tradition of serving the Tsars at war, they were destined to be hopelessly wide of the mark. Yet the Pyotr in this generation was to be the first to bring his family recognition that went far beyond the boundaries of the Russian upper middle-class. Ilya's mother had borne twenty children. Life was not to be quite such a production line for Alexandra, but two years after Pyotr she had a daughter whom she named after herself and then three more sons, Ippolit in 1843, then the twins Modest and Anatoly in 1850. Pyotr's first years were spent in a secure and happy family, with a father known for his affection and sentimental generosity. Though money was not lavishly available, his father earned a decent salary and the house that accompanied the job meant that they lived in considerable comfort.

When Pyotr, or 'Petya' as he was called in the family, was four his mother left him for four months to travel to St Petersburg. There were three good reasons for the trip: she wanted to see her own family, she needed to visit her step-daughter Zinaida who was fifteen and had been sent to boarding school – the Ekaterinsky Institute – in the capital, and she realised that a family in their position required a governess if the children

Alexandra Alexeyvna
Tchaikovskaya (1813-1854),
Pyotr's mother, pictured in 1848.

were to grow up with the sort of education that would allow them to mix in a more cosmopolitan society than that of Votkinsk. Nicholai went with her on the trip but the three younger children, Petya, Alexandra and the baby Ippolit, stayed at home. For Petya, parting from his mother was always to be traumatic and it is revealing that his reaction to it on this occasion was to compose a little song.

Alexandra Andreyevna returned home in November 1844, bringing with her Fanny Durbach, the governess. Her duties were to take charge not only of Nicolai and Pyotr's education but also that of their cousin Lidiya. As they grew older her class came to include other children who came within the Tchaikovsky orbit, like Venichka Alexeyev, the son of one of Ilya's staff. Fanny was only 22 when she arrived in Votkinsk, a French girl with a strictly Protestant view of the world. The similarity of her background to Alexandra's own must have made her an easy choice for her 30-year-old employer.

Not surprisingly Fanny was apprehensive and frightened of the isolation of living in Votkinsk but the Tchaikovskies were a sensitive family and Ilya embraced her like a daughter when she arrived. It was a feeling of welcome that stayed with her throughout the four years she spent with them, to be remembered as among the happiest of her life. This was not just a matter of an elderly lady looking back in retirement on her years with her most famous charge. When Modest Tchaikovsky went to see Fanny in France after his brother's death to gather memories, he found that her time in the Tchaikovsky household had genuinely been remarkably carefree. Perhaps Ilya's warm liberality is best expressed in Fanny's memory of her surprise that when she arrived she found that:

It was difficult to distinguish family from servants in the crowd. All were made one by an undivided, living joy... I had not just arrived; rather, like Mme Tchaikovskaya and her son, I too had 'returned home'.

She was put in complete charge of the children for most of the day, joining Ilya and Alexandra only for meals. She instituted a strict regime, beginning every morning at six. Mornings were given over to lessons. In the afternoons Fanny encouraged the children to get as much exercise as possible and in the summer they were sometimes lent the family carriage to explore the countryside around Votkinsk. In the evening they read and talked in their own nursery quarters or took part in the wider family entertainments. She found the boys very different from one another. Nicholai was handsome and well turned-out but not inclined to work harder than necessary and was often in minor trouble for some misdemeanour or other. Pyotr (or Pierre as she called him, sticking firmly to her role as the French governess) was more messy in his appearance but rarely had to be reprimanded. He was also a diligent little boy, more interested in his lessons, quicker on the uptake than his older relations and had an inventive gift for storytelling. His obvious intelligence and his pleasure in learning made him an easy pupil, to the extent that he was able to read in Russian, French and German at the age of six and write creditable French verses reflecting the stories they read together at seven.

Petya had two strong memories that stayed with him from these early years. One was of his first trip away from Votkinsk. When he was five his mother took him and his cousin Anastasia on a trip to the spa town of Sergiyevsk, nearly three hundred miles further down the Volga. It was a magical journey, not least because it gave him his first and, as it turned out, one of his only chances to spend time alone with his mother. The other

The Tchaikovsky family, so rarely together, in 1848 before the twins were born. Eight-year-old Pyotr stands on the left. Zinaida has her arm round her step-mother's shoulder, Ippolit sits on his father's knee, Nicholai stands as the young man, Sasha is having trouble staying still and looks bored to distraction.

was his joy and relief at seeing his mother again the next year after both parents had been away for nearly four months, leaving the 24-year-old Fanny in charge. They had gone to St Petersburg partly on Ilya's business but mainly to collect Zinaida when she graduated from school. It is a measure of the severity of the education system then that the six-year-old Petya had never met his seventeen-year-old half-sister. She had been incarcerated in the boarding school since before he was born.

Zinaida charmed him with her prettiness and teenage sophistication. But Petya had great charm too and knew how to touch the hearts of those around him. Allied to his imaginative fertility, though, was a strain of over-sensitivity which could send him into torments of anxiety or remorse over the slightest hint of a scold. He was no timid flower though, and often his outbursts would be on behalf of one of the other children, Venichka Alexeyev or Nicholai, whom he felt had been treated unfairly, or an animal that deserved a reprieve. Music had an effect on him that Fanny thought quite disastrous. It emphasised his highly-strung side and she disapproved of his preference for playing the piano after morning lessons rather than running about outside with the others. There is a famous anecdote about Petya being unable to settle or sleep after an evening of domestic music with his parents (Alexandra sang well and played the harp) and their guests, crying that the music in his head wouldn't give him any peace.

When, sometime in 1845 or early 1846 Maria Palchikova, another of the household staff, started to offer some proper piano lessons Fanny opposed it and it seems it was only when Petya had put his hand through a window by trying to tap out a tune on the glass that his parents decided that Fanny should on this occasion be overruled. There were no orchestral concerts to be heard in Votkinsk – at that date there were very few even in St Petersburg – but Ilya Tchaikovsky was the proud possessor of an 'orchestrion', a grand music box that used printed cards to play a set of organ pipes in imitation of a full orchestra. For young Pyotr it was a delight and gave him his first experience of the music of Mozart (extracts from *Don Giovanni*), Rossini, Bellini and Donizetti. This exposure to the Italian composers had a remarkably lasting effect on both his taste and mature style. It was also a tribute to the music industry of the 1840s that it could disseminate the work of contemporary musicians to the furthest reaches of Europe without all the modern advantages of radio and recording. Chopin was also to be heard, played by a Polish resident of the town named

A letter from Pyotr to Fanny Durbach in 1848. The fluency of the writing and the ease of the French would now be seen as quite extraordinary in an eight-year-old.

Chère Mlle Fanny,

Je ne puis vous dire comme j'étais content, quand j'ai reçu votre lettre; je vous prie chère Mlle Fanny ne vous fachez pas contre moi; vous me dites, que vous avez pleuré, de ce que je vous ai écrit, que c'est ma paresse qui m'a empêché de vous écrire; je tacherai une autrefois de ne jamais être paresseux, car je conviens que c'est un mauvais sentiment, dont je me corrigerai. A présent, je veux vous va conter, comment j'ai passé le temps le 20 de Juillet, le jour de fête de papa. Monsieur Zélénzoff M. Tchaikovsky et Monsieur Penn avec ses deux filles Suzanne et Alice étaient arrivés chez nous. Le soir

Maszewski who had a fine repertoire of mazurkas. Duly impressed, Petya learned to play two himself, a feat that earned him a kiss from the musician and left him 'never so contented as on that day' as Fanny reported.

The contentment did not last long. In 1848 Ilya Tchaikovsky decided that eleven years in Votkinsk was enough and that his career needed a boost which only a return to a major city could provide. At the age of fifty-two the frustration was understandable but whatever qualities he possessed as a manager, his judgement in exchanging the security and relative splendour of his position at the summit of Votkinsk society for a much more uncertain future was thoroughly suspect. Although his early retirement from Government service earned him the pseudo-military rank of Major-General, with four children to support between the ages of four and nineteen, risking everything on the prospect of an uncertain new job was a decision that was less than inspired. As Sir Landon Ronald put it in an early essay on the composer, 'in Russia you either hold an official position or you are nobody.'

Nonetheless in September the whole family was uprooted and transported to Moscow. Pyotr left his closest friend, Venichka, behind and Fanny was dismissed after four years of service in which she had proved to be an exceptional teacher and an irreplaceable source of authority for the children. For the eight-year-old Pyotr the wrench was traumatic and far-reaching. He was never as settled or as happy again as he had been at Votkinsk.

The whole venture seemed doomed from the start. Nicholai and Pyotr were enrolled in a school as soon as they reached Moscow but stayed for little more than a month. Ilya's new job, for which he had given up so much and of which he was so confident, evaporated. It seems he had rashly mentioned the prospect to a colleague who promptly and successfully manoeuvred to secure it for himself. Ilya then tried to regain the initiative by making for St Petersburg, leaving the household in the care of Alexandra and Zinaida. The latter did not relish looking after her two young half-brothers and, of the two, preferred the more even-keeled Nicholai to the fraught Pyotr who was reacting to the upheavals of the autumn by being unwontedly difficult.

In November they too abandoned Moscow for St Petersburg, no doubt much to the relief of Zinaida. As far as Pyotr was concerned, however, it was not much of an improvement and he wrote increasingly despairing letters to Fanny yearning for the old life in Votkinsk. The boys were in truth having a miserable time. They had been sent to a fashionable school, the Schmelling, as day boys. They arrived in the middle of the winter term, having had their work badly interrupted by the departure of Fanny and the unsatisfactory period in Moscow. Their only experience of school had been during the previous weeks and that had been to a different curriculum. To catch up they sometimes had to work on their homework until midnight, having started the school day at eight in the morning. In between they were bullied by the other boys for their country ways and unfamiliarity with school life. It was too much for both of them and within a few weeks they succumbed to measles.

The winter was grim and for Major-General Tchaikovsky the full force of his mistake in giving up his privileged position in Votkinsk for a late middle-age of unemployment in St Petersburg must have been hard to take. When Nicholai recovered from measles he was sent not to the unsatisfactory Schmelling School but to his father's alma mater, the School of Mine Engineering. For Nicholai this proved to be the right choice and during 1849 he settled in well. For Pyotr, though, recovery took longer. After measles he was said to be suffering from a spinal infection and any return to school was ruled out for an indefinite period.

Given his sensitivity and his passionate need to be close to his family, it is hardly surprising that his body came up with some ailment to make sure he stayed at home. If there were compensations they were musical. His enforced rest meant that he had the time to take his first piano lessons from a professional teacher, a man named Fillipov. He was also taken to see the opera and apparently the ballet too, though it seems that he was either too young or too ill for these performances to make any lasting impression beyond an awareness of the thrill of the theatre.

A respite of sorts for the family came in the spring of 1849 when Ilya Tchaikovsky at last found a new job. His mistake in leaving the old one was made starkly apparent by the comparison with a year before. He was appointed manager of the mines and metal works at Alapayevsk. Unlike Votkinsk, where the plant was state-owned and carried with it an Imperial position, that at Alapayevsk was a private concern. It was nothing like as extensive or as prestigious and the town itself reflected this minor status. If Votkinsk had seemed provincial, Alapayevsk was much worse. It lay on the other side of the Ural Mountains, north of Ekaterinburg (to be made famous seventy years later as the site of the assassination of Tsar Nicholas II and his family) and was only just in the province of Perm where European Russia officially ended and the swampy plains of Siberia began. The Tchaikovsky family moved from St Petersburg and they settled in during June. In local terms Ilya's position was important and the house that went with the job was spacious and comfortable, yet there was nothing like the social life of Votkinsk and even less artistic activity – and Votkinsk had hardly been overflowing with it.

For Pyotr the alternative was worse but he badly missed his old life. Zinaida was no adequate replacement for Fanny

Durbach (and the 20-year-old must have been bored to tears in Alapayevsk). Nicholai was missing, doing well back in St Petersburg. Lidiya was still with them, as were Sasha and Ippolit, the two younger children, and another cousin, Amalia Schobert, soon joined them but Pyotr, at nine, wanted the company of boys and there was no Venichka to keep him company. Neither was there a decent music teacher. He had outgrown the abilities of Maria Palchikova who returned to the family the following year and all he could really achieve was some practice on his own.

In the autumn of 1849 his mother became pregnant again and in December, after what must have been an arduous journey across the mountains at that time of year, a new

The original 1836 set for Glinka's *A Life for the Tsar*. By the time Tchaikovsky saw the opera in 1849 the production was past its best but it still had a life-long influence.

governess arrived to take over the children from Zinaida's inexpert care. For Anastasia Petrova, at 25 and without parents of her own, the prospect of being thrown into a family in such a remote region, connected with the rougher side of industrial production, must have seemed daunting. Ilya Tchaikovsky soon pulled off his trick of making people feel at home, however, and Anastasia proved to be a capable and sympathetic teacher.

The Pyotr she had in hand was not, though, the young charmer that Fanny had known. The last eighteen months, in which his world had been dismantled and reassembled far from intact, had left their mark on his character. He had always been abnormally sensitive to criticism but now that was allied with touchiness and a tendency to answer back. His old zest for learning, which had made him such a model pupil for Fanny, had gone and instead Anastasia had to work hard to make up for the lost momentum in his education. This was becoming important, for his parents had decided that he should join Nicholai at boarding school in the autumn of 1850, by which time he would be ten and a half. Meanwhile, though, in May twin brothers, Anatoly and Modest, were born. Their safe arrival and his liking for Anastasia seemed to lift Pyotr out of his slump and the summer with his sisters, brothers and cousins was more like the old days.

He did not have long to enjoy the new security, however, as he well knew. Anastasia's task was not just to carry on where Fanny had left off but to bring Pyotr up to the standard expected at his new school. Originally the intention had been that he should follow Nicholai to the Mining School but at some time during the year his parents changed their minds, perhaps realising that unlike his brother and father, Pyotr was not by nature interested in such practical matters. The decision had nothing to do with music, however, for the school provided a

The Winter Palace in St. Petersburg. Throughout his life the only city which impressed Tchaikovsky as much was Paris.

good general education for gentlemen on the fringes of the nobility and Nicholai himself was making steady progress in his piano studies as much as in the rest of the curriculum. Whatever the reason, Ilya settled on the School of Jurisprudence as the appropriate route into government service for Pyotr. He could enter the main school when he was 12 but it had a preparatory school attached and he passed the entrance exam for that and enrolled in September, having set out with his mother, Zinaida and Sasha from Alapayevsk in the second week of August. For Alexandra Andreyevna it cannot have felt like good timing, for it meant leaving the twins, only three months old, with a wet nurse for almost the rest of the year.

Soon after they had arrived in St Petersburg Mme Tchaikovskaya gave her son a taste of the joys of city life when she took him to see *A Life for the Tsar*, Glinka's first opera, premiered in 1836. Although the production was inadequate, it was not enough to discourage a child as naturally musical as Pyotr, and the event was remembered and digested long enough for the work to become a strong influence on his own operas 20 years later.

Life at the School of Jurisprudence Prep was a good deal better than it had been at the Schmelling School the year before, though it was known for its strict discipline. The school week was six days long with the children allowed home on Sundays. Since 'home' in the case of the Tchaikovsky boys was as far away from St Petersburg as Shetland, a friend of Ilya's, Modest Vakar (after whom the young twin was probably named in thanks) had undertaken to look after them and act *in loco parentis*. This at least meant that Nicholai and Pyotr, though not at the same school (as they had thought they would be), could spend a few days each month and the holidays together.

1850, though, was to end as miserably for Pyotr as 1849 had done. For the first few weeks of term Alexandra had stayed with the Vakars to make sure that he was established at school and to see something of Nicholai, whom she had not seen for well over a year. By October, however, it was clear that she would have to return home to the twins before winter made the journey even more unpleasant than it was usually. Zinaida and Sasha were to go home too. Nicholai and Pyotr, along with Zinaida's maternal uncle Ilya, accompanied them as far as the turnpike on the road to Moscow. The boys' father had predicted that parting for an indefinite and, for a child, unimaginable period, would be particularly hard on Pyotr and he was more right than he would have wished. When the time

Tsar Nicholas I (1796-1855), the autocrat who prevented political and social reform in Russia.

came to say goodbye Pyotr would not let go of his mother and had to be pulled away, screaming. Even when the carriage had set off he ran after it, trying desperately to catch hold of any part that would stop it from taking her away. For any child it can be a traumatic moment but for Pyotr, who had seen all the security he had enjoyed in his early years systematically destroyed and for whom his mother was more important than anyone or anything else, this forced separation was the last straw. He never forgot or overcame its agony, even in middle age, and it is arguable that it was the root of much of his neurosis in later life.

Within a few weeks his sense of abandonment was increased by a real tragedy which he unwittingly instigated. An outbreak of scarlet fever put the school in quarantine. Pyotr was allowed to live with the Vakar family, instead of remaining in school, until the danger was past. Given the inadequacy of epidemiology in Russia then, it was an unwise decision and Modest Vakar's pity on the boy was bitterly tested when his own son contracted the disease as a direct result of Pyotr's return and died early in December. In the few weeks he had known him Pyotr had become very attached to the five-year-old Kolya and despite the family's attempts to shield Pyotr from the blame – he had, after all, no control over the decision – Nicholai Vakar's death added guilt to the list of emotions bringing him distress.

During the winter Pyotr's hopes were raised that his father, at least, would visit him in February but he was unable to leave the mines in Alapayevsk and the visit was postponed until the summer. Pyotr reacted with predictable desperation. His letters home were torrents of endearment and misery anyway, but at moments like this he was especially adept at turning up the emotional pressure on his parents:

'...if, my beautiful angels, you do not come, then we shall be very lonely. I think your dear hearts will take pity on us and that you'll come... we shall expect you in June without fail!'

He was aware that the prospect of being reunited with his parents meant more to him than to Nicholai, who was clearly well settled in at his school, but that only seemed to increase the unfairness of it all. When his eleventh birthday arrived on 7 May 1851, he greeted it with tears, admitting that he 'cried a lot when I remembered the happy time I spent last year in Alapayevsk, but', he went on, 'I had two friends with me, Belyavsky and Dokhturov, who comforted me.'

In fact one has to draw a line of circumspection between the reality of school life and the demonstration of overwrought emotions in the letters, of which Pyotr wrote about one every four or five days. By the standards of the mid-nineteenth century he was not treated badly, indeed his form teacher, Joseph Berrard, who taught literature and French, went out of his way to make sure the sensitive boy was given the support he needed. He seems to have been popular with the other boys, who enjoyed his fooling around at the piano, and Pyotr joined in their games readily enough. He was not all angelic, either; he developed his taste for practical jokes which lasted a lifetime and although he ranked third in his exams after Christmas he was kept in on one Sunday a few weeks later for laziness, for which he apologised to his parents, though one suspects that the 'distress' was not theirs but his.

The entertainments of life in the empire's principal city were not completely closed to him either. During the course of his time at prep school he went to the opera and the ballet, seeing among other things Adam's *Giselle*. In April 1851 he went with his classmates to a children's ball, held in the presence of the Tsar. Nicholai I was 55 and had ruled Russia with ferocity for quarter of a century. He was a tall and handsome man and a rigid militarist whose accession had been bitterly opposed by many. He had responded by becoming the most reactionary ruler the country had had in two hundred years. He had stopped the modernisation of Russian society, had stifled any attempts to continue the reforms instituted by his brother, Alexander I, and kept the majority of his people in mediaeval conditions of feudalism which had died out in the rest of Europe half a millennium earlier. If the inability of the Russian people to find a stable and moderate form of civilised government can be traced to anyone, it is to Nicholai I. For the young Pyotr Tchaikovsky, however, seeing him for the first time at a ball was an appropriately impressive occasion and he was happy enough to go away with the toy soldier he won in the raffle. In one sense, though, his reaction was a harbinger of things to come, for even in adult life he never showed more than a passing interest in politics and was content to enjoy the social glamour that the court dispensed.

In May 1851 Modest Vakar and his family left the capital and responsibility for the care of the two Tchaikovsky boys was passed to his brother, Platon, a graduate of the School of Jurisprudence himself, who therefore had some idea of what Pyotr was experiencing. As had been half expected, the June visit of Ilya did not materialise, so Nicholai and Pyotr were taken to spend their six week summer holiday with some relatives in the country. While Pyotr still missed his own family surroundings, being in the country at all was the next best thing.

In the event Ilya Tchaikovsky finally managed to come to St Petersburg in the second week of September 1851, in time to settle the boys back into school and to have Pyotr with him in his lodgings for the best part of a month. The job in Alapayevsk was proving to be as unsatisfactory for him as it was for the rest of the family. He had come to St Petersburg to bring matters to a head with the company management and during the course of his visit he handed in his notice. He was no longer a young man, though, and at the age of 56, with three sons and a daughter still to start in education (and the school fees for Nicholai and Pyotr to count as well), it cannot have been a decision lightly taken. The Tchaikovsky family was not poor but they had no significant independent means and some form of income was necessary. Nonetheless, he was resolved that he had had enough of the Ural provinces and that the move he had originally tried to make three years before had been the right one.

Closing up in Alapayevsk and transporting the household was not an easy matter, however, and Ilya's hopes that it could all be accomplished by the end of the year proved to be wildly optimistic. Still, Pyotr's hopes had been raised and when it became clear the reunion would have to be put off until the spring, the disappointment seemed just to be a continuation of all those he had suffered over the previous eighteen months. From everybody else's point of view, however, it would have been less than sensible to trek across Russia with two toddlers and all the family belongings in the middle of winter, even though one part of the journey was revolutionised that year with the opening of the St Petersburg to Moscow railway. So in the meantime Platon and Maria Vakar continued to offer a foster home to the boys when they were not at school.

The rest of the Tchaikovsky family returned from the Urals in May 1852. For Pyotr the delayed timing was good in one respect – it meant he was in a positive frame of mind for the exams that he had to take that month in order to move up to the senior forms of the School of Jurisprudence. He passed commendably and for the first time in two years he was able to set off for the summer holidays in the company of the full family, complete with cousins. Ilya Tchaikovsky seems to have realised the importance of the family reunion to them all and he took a villa north of the city, on the Black River (close to

Lake Ladoga and Finland) so that they could all be together in the country.

The feeling of a return to normality made Pyotr much more like his old self and he spent the summer, the last of his real childhood, plaguing his cousins with practical jokes and revelling in the freedom away from the strict discipline of his prep school. The contentment continued into the autumn when he returned to St Petersburg for the start of his first term in the main part of the School of Jurisprudence. The knowledge that all his family were within walking distance – indeed he could look into his aunt's house from the school dormitory window – made all the difference to him and he soon settled in well. The proximity of his aunt – his mother's sister Ekaterina Alexeyeva – came to have musical importance too. She was the most musical member of the family and introduced Pyotr to Rossini arias and the full piano score of *Don Giovanni*, which he later came to regard as a critical moment in his own musical development.

With four years in the junior school and three in the senior ahead of him he was entering a world from which he was expected to emerge as a fully-qualified candidate for ministerial service, a gentleman with the potential to join the nobility and a Russian capable of being among the elite of his own country and linguistically and socially equipped to mix with the best anywhere in the world. The School had grand buildings overlooking the city's Summer Garden and it enjoyed the direct patronage of the Royal family. Pyotr Illych was a privileged boy in a country of intense poverty and deprivation.

One aspect that gave him immediate personal status and self-confidence was his inclusion in the school choir as soon as he arrived. At last his musical ability was recognised by more than his family and fellow pupils. There was no thought of music as a profession, as yet – there was, in 1852, almost no such thing in Russia outside the few players at the Imperial Opera and it certainly would not have been considered an acceptable career to aim for at a school so intricately connected with supplying civil servants for Nicholai I's blinkered government.

There was no official place for music in the school curriculum, though it seems there had been a few years earlier before the Tsar's purge of liberal ideas in the education system. The school had in fact already produced two men who became central figures in the country's musical development; the writer and critic, Vladimir Stasov and the composer Alexander Serov, who had left the school the year Tchaikovsky was born. The latter could have been held up as the perfect example of why music was not considered a suitable career for graduates. At the time Tchaikovsky arrived in the school, Serov had just given up an unexciting, but at least paid, legal post in the provinces and was trying to eke out a living in St Petersburg through writing articles and attempting to write opera. If it had not been for the most musical member of the royal family, the Grand Duchess Elena Pavlovna, he would probably have slipped from shabby eccentricity into total destitution.

However if music rarely led to comfortable employment, it was taken seriously as a social attribute for anybody with a decent upbringing and a solid knowledge of the music associated with the Orthodox Church was part of that. Indeed the Church was integral to the Imperial idea of Russian statehood, just as it was in its counterpart empires in Britain and Austro-Hungary. The school choir was instructed by Gavriil Lomakin, who was on the staff of the Imperial Chapel. In general voices broke later among boys than they do now and so for Pyotr's first three years he remained a treble. His competence was soon recognised when he was made the lead second treble, perhaps the most demanding job in the choir because he had to give a firm sense of direction to the less talented singers who were put in his charge.

1853 was one of the most balanced years of Tchaikovsky's life. He came to terms with the discipline of school, managing to avoid the savage beatings that were considered an exemplary part of an education by the Director, an ex-chief of police in Latvia. His sensitivity, which was never combined with the drippiness that would have brought him derision, made him well-liked by his fellow boys and by his form master, Ivan Samoylovich Alopeus. Ilya Tchaikovsky was now properly retired and supporting the family as best he could on his pension and the proceeds of investments. Zinaida, now 24, was being seriously courted by Evgeny Olkhovsky. It was something of a double solution for Lidiya, the cousin who had lived with them since childhood, was conveniently paired with Evgeny's elder bother, Nicholai. In January 1854 Zinaida and Evgeny were married and, in what she must have been becoming resigned to as the pattern of her life, promptly returned with him to the Urals.

The happy stability was short-lived, however and the reason for its removal could not have been more devastating for Pyotr. At the beginning of the summer his mother contracted cholera. As a disease cholera could hardly be more distressing, with its sudden and intense onset, its associated diarrhoea, vomiting and dehydration and, in 1854, there was inadequate knowledge to combat it. Because it is transmitted orally it is also highly contagious. The simple remedies of plenty of fluid, salt and sodium chloride were all available but unknown to the doctors and there were no antibiotics to fight the infection. Patients usually died delirious, exhausted and literally drained within a week. When Alexandra Tchaikovskaya fell ill the children were sent to Ekaterina's, out of reach of the infected house. For a few days, Pyotr remembered two years later when he at last found the composure to write about it to Fanny Durbach, his mother rallied. It became clear though that the respite was only temporary and Pyotr and Sasha were called to her bedside on 13 June. Twelve-year-old Ippolit in turn broke out and ran across the city to join them but he was too late. As Pyotr recalled, Alexandra Andreyevna died without being able to say goodbye. She was only 41.

Chapter 2

In the Legal System

For all the family Alexandra's death was a tragedy difficult to come to terms with. At 59 Ilya found himself alone with the responsibility for six children between the ages of 16 and four. The twins, Anatoly and Modest, were left with only fleeting memories of their mother (which was, at least, more than Zinaida had of hers). It was the three middle children, Pyotr, Sasha and Ippolit, who were at the most vulnerable ages, however, and they never completely recovered from the shock.

Ilya Tchaikovsky with his twins, Modest and Anatoly, in 1855.

Pyotr himself could barely talk about it for years and even he realised that much of his later emotional chaos had its roots in that day. He was old enough to have every moment of it etched into his consciousness, too young to be able, as his father and elder brother eventually were, to detach himself from the sense of sudden desertion. The summer holidays, in such stark contrast to the carefree childish rampage of the year before, were utterly desolate.

The immediate effect was to throw him into a search of his emotional resources. At 14 he was beginning to explore his own expressive world and the death of his mother became a catalyst. Whereas before he had been content to enjoy music as a singer and pianist, he wanted now to compose. As so often in his life, however, the musical subject matter and his emotional state at the time bear no strong relationship to each other. Tchaikovsky is often thought of as the perfect example of the late romantic composer, pouring out his most tortured feelings in music. He did this on many occasions but like all great artists his work did not always react with such convenient timing for the biographer; instead the emotional impulse would be stored away and emerge later, better formed. So after his mother's death in 1854 he did not embark on a tragic symphony or a morbid cantata. That summer – when Ilya had taken the family to recover at Oranienbaum, 25 miles east of St Petersburg on the Gulf of Finland – Pyotr wrote a waltz and dedicated it to Anastasia Petrova, the governess who had prepared him for his entrance exams five years before. The *Anastasia Valse* is his first composition to survive.

Fired by the experience of writing, he wanted to tackle something more substantial and asked Zinaida's brother-in-law, Victor Olkhovsky, who had some reputation as a poet, for an opera libretto. He responded by sending a one-act piece called *Hyperbole*, with which the young composer was delighted but complained that it contained too many arias and recitatives. Not only did he want to be a composer, it seemed, he wanted to be a radical one. By the time he received it, however, the school year had begun again and, as was often to happen in the future, this opera project went no further.

Ilya Tchaikovsky responded to his wife's death by trying to rebuild family life. It was not easy. Zinaida had gone, his niece Lidiya married after the summer and it was time for Sasha and Ippolit to enter full-time schooling (the later entering the Naval Academy). That left only the young twins at home. To fill what must have seemed a dreadful gap he called on his 66-year-old elder brother Pyotr Petrovich and his family to move in with them, which they did, staying for three years. This extension of the family added five girls to the household, along with Pyotr Petrovich's jolly wife Elisaveta. One of the daughters, Anna who was then 24, had already spent the previous summer with them (she was very attached to Lidiya and Zinaida) and became particularly fond of Pyotr, remaining one of his closest confidants for the rest of his life. By the time they moved in Uncle Pyotr was deeply eccentric, having long retired from his distinguished military life. He spent most of his time in the study writing mystical pamphlets and emerging for long walks on which he delivered sweets, as a gift from heaven to any child he happened to pass along the way – a habit which his nephew was also to adopt later in life. This gently dotty old man and his ebullient dependants were a rich source of comfort to the bereft Ilya and his children.

School seemed to have a calming effect on Pyotr. Perhaps now that he had no mother to run home to, or who could be held up as an idol from a better country life, and that he was among his friends of several years' standing in an institution he had come to know and operate within, school seemed as close to normal life as he was going to get. The class to which he belonged had a reputation for being particularly unruly, even by the standards of those days, which Alopeus, the form teacher, did not always succeed in keeping under control. The following year, 1855, Alopeus was promoted to the post of Inspector – effectively that of Deputy Head – which alleviated the sense of terror that the previous incumbent, a vicious ex-Colonel called Rutenburg, had cultivated. His replacement in the life of the form was the grand-sounding Baron Prosper Gaillard de Baccarat, vague and, it seems, professionally barely adequate even at teaching his native French. Plainly he regarded teaching as beneath his dignity, though not so demeaning that the income could be ignored. The death of Tsar Nicholai I that year and the succession of Alexander II, as liberal as his father had been brutal, may well have contributed to the less oppressive atmosphere which, percolating through St Petersburg, touched even the closed world of the school.

There Pyotr was beginning to draw together his circle of friends from outside the family. Foremost among them were Fyodor Maslov and Vladimir Gerard (both of whom went on to join the legal profession for which they were preparing), Vladimir Adamov and Alexei Apukhtin. Maslov was delicate for his age, pale and thin, a characteristic which Tchaikovsky was always to find sympathetic, and in the sixth and seventh forms Maslov himself describes themselves as being 'almost

My genius, my angel, my friend, the manuscript of one of three songs written around 1855, the first of Tchaikovsky's surviving compositions.

inseparable'. His description of Tchaikovsky at school is particularly vivid and, given Pyotr's love of practical jokes and Fanny Durbach's account of his childhood anarchic energy, rings thoroughly true:

'In his daily life he was distinguished for his disorderliness and untidiness. He filched nearly all his father's library for his comrades but when he himself used the books of others he did not bother to return them. ... Pyotr Illych never had his own textbooks and tried to borrow them from his comrades. But his own desk was also, as it were, on open access and whoever wanted could rummage in it. In his later years at school Tchaikovsky kept a diary entitled *Everything*, where he

29

poured out all the secrets of his soul, but was so naively trusting that he did not keep it under lock but in that same desk lying in the general pile of his own and others' books and exercise books.'

Maslov also remembered the time when they strolled out into the Summer Garden to revise for the school exams and, to save the trouble of taking everything with them each time, hid their notes in the hollow of a tree. Maslov duly retrieved his but Tchaikovsky never got round to it and, as far as his friends knew, they could have been rotting there years later. Gerard too remembered Tchaikovsky as fundamentally absent-minded.

The creative drive which appeared after his mother's death seems to have become dormant again once the routine of school life reasserted itself. This does not mean music was neglected, however, merely that he was not writing any of his own and it did not take up a disproportionate amount of his time. He still sang in the choir, even when his voice had broken. In 1855 he also began to take more demanding music lessons again. These were given privately by a young German pianist called Rudolph Kündinger and later, for theory, by his brother Auguste. Tchaikovsky's piano technique improved dramatically and he enjoyed exhibiting his skill to his friends, either playing with the keyboard covered by a towel or by extemporising on the harmonium after choir rehearsals, producing variations on any tune that was thrown at him. It was this talent for improvisation and, despite his ignorance of music theory, his instinct for harmony that gave his teacher pause for thought and marked him as out of the ordinary. However Kündinger was not so impressed that he regarded the boy as a potential professional when the subject was broached to him by his father – who had always supported Pyotr's musical enthusiasms and, even as early as this, seems to have realised that a lawyer's life was unlikely to suit him for long. The teacher later candidly gave two reasons for discouraging the idea of abandoning law for music:

'in the first place because I did not see in Pyotr Illych the genius that subsequently manifested itself, and secondly because I myself experienced how hard was the lot of a professional musician in Russia at that time. ... Certainly his abilities were notable: a strikingly fine ear, memory, an outstanding hand, but all this gave no cause to foresee in him even a brilliant performer, let alone a composer. There was nothing surprising in this: before and since Tchaikovsky I have had occasion to meet not infrequently young people with such gifts.'

The lessons took place every Sunday morning when Pyotr was allowed home from school. His teacher stayed on for lunch with the family afterwards; not an unpleasant duty for the 23-year-old, given the number of female Tchaikovskies that were gathered there too. After lunch he and Pyotr would go off to the concerts at the university, somewhat lackadaisical affairs given by enthusiastic amateurs without the benefit of a rehearsal but at that time the only regular series in St Petersburg and, at five roubles for a season ticket, reasonably within the price range of those of limited means.

Tchaikovsky's emotional life at this period seems to have been as turbulent as – or perhaps no more turbulent than – that of most teenage boys in the single sex environment of nineteenth-century boarding schools. The homosexuality which came to be so dominant in his twenties and thirties does not seem to have manifested itself more than it did with many of the other boys. He may have had a crush on Fyodor Maslov – certainly Vladimir Taneyev (brother of the composer Sergei), who was in the form below and later became virtually homophobic, did – and possibly later on Gerard, although there is no firm evidence that these went any further than adolescent obsessions. Neither Maslov nor Gerard was overtly homosexual in later life and Gerard mentions that he and Tchaikovsky spent plenty of time and effort discussing girls in their last years at the school. Alexei Apukhtin was a different matter, however. He was the literary 'star' of the school, editing the pupils' newspaper and even in his early teens showing the poetic talent which made his fellows hold him in intellectual awe. His mind had a swagger to it which easily impressed not only the boys but the school authorities as well and even figures in Russia's literary establishment like Turgenev.

Apukhtin's advent in the class in 1853 broke the intimacy between Maslov and Tchaikovsky when, returning from a spell in the sick bay, Maslov found his place at the desk with his best friend taken by Apukhtin. Normally among thirteen-year-olds this would have been little more than a changeover of 'best friends' but Apukhtin and Tchaikovsky retained their closeness throughout their school years and well into their twenties. The young poet quickly acquired a girl's nickname, 'Lyolya', and he had the sickly, pallid constitution that Tchaikovsky usually favoured later, almost as if he was always looking for the sort of substitute girls that were to be found at school. Tchaikovsky was a close companion, contributing to the school paper that Apukhtin edited and, from the age of fifteen on, becoming the subject of poems which are full of deep tenderness, though not

The building which in
Tchaikovsky's time housed the
School of Jurisprudence. In the
foreground is the River
Fontanka.

full-scale love. He was, however, one of several boys in the school of whom this could have been said and, given Apukhtin's demonstrative style and the way he used his experiences as extendible source material for his poetry, the writing tells us more about his relationship with Tchaikovsky than it does about Tchaikovsky's seemingly more detached view of him. Apukhtin was, in any case, hard to get along with for long but Tchaikovsky was a tolerant person who valued friendship highly, however it was expressed, and who appreciated the depth and range of Apukhtin's conversation as much as the intensity of his emotional life. He also valued his criticism of creative efforts which, for the most part at this stage of Tchaikovsky's life, still took the form of poetry rather than music, as they had done in childhood.

There were other friends too, older – like Prince Vladimir Meshchersky – and younger – like Sergei Kireyev, for whom Tchaikovsky held feelings at some time in his years at school which went beyond the usual limits of platonic affection. Given the inevitable caution to be found in documentary evidence it is difficult to go much further than this. However it is reasonable to assume that anything written down in a letter to a third party or as a memoir will underplay the true extent of sexual attraction except where it was regarded at the time as socially legitimate. In 1850s Russia a bit of exploration between boys was tolerated and, although not encouraged, was not seen as dangerous as long as it was not continued into adulthood. Since Tchaikovsky went to great and disastrous lengths to keep his homosexuality private later, he was not likely to encourage talk of early liaisons with people like Meschersky and Apukhtin, neither of whom were regarded as having acceptable lifestyles. It is fair to assume, then, that Tchaikovsky's homosexual experience did start at the School of Jurisprudence and that it was well developed by the time he left. It would not be fair to assume, however, that he was not attracted to women at this stage or that he regarded himself as being exclusively interested in men. That realisation may not have come until the appalling failure of his marriage 20 years later. In his teens Tchaikovsky – ever-generous with his emotions – was wide and free with his fantasy and affection.

If the School of Jurisprudence was proving fertile ground for emotional complication, there is no doubt that in other respects it was giving him an excellent education. He was not excelling in the way that he had under the concentrated tutelage of Fanny Durbach and Alexandra Petrova – much of that precocious brilliance would re-emerge when he needed it for composition – but he was able to mature in an intellectual environment dedicated to training the best legal and official brains in the country. But the authorities knew that to graduate into the elite of society more than a knowledge of law was needed. So the boys were encouraged to develop their cultural faculties in the emerging sophistication of St Petersburg.

Once the police-state regime of Tsar Nicholai I was superseded in 1855, the atmosphere became more liberal and Russia began to explore simultaneously the expression of nationalism that had gathered force elsewhere in Europe after the upheavals of 1848 and to open its cities more to the tastes and ideas of western Europe, especially France. So Tchaikovsky and his companions, particularly Gerard and Maslov, would frequent the opera and theatre. The former was almost entirely Italian and dated from the previous 30 years, with a strong bias towards Donizzetti, Rossini and Bellini. Mozart was occasionally available as was the home-grown Glinka. It was presented in the Bolshoi Theatre, by the time Tchaikovsky and his friends began to frequent it equipped with a fine new interior after a major fire in 1853. In the homes and social circle of the aristocracy there was private music-making of a very high standard, to which no doubt some of the boys had access. For public consumption, though, the Imperial opera offered the only decent standard of professional musicianship. In Lent the theatres were closed and this freed the players and singers of the Imperial staff to use the concert platform. In 1850, perhaps weary of the unrehearsed amateur efforts at the university, a group of enthusiasts formed a Concert Society to provide orchestral and chamber music in more polished performances. Until it was formed, the main concerts had been provided by the Philharmonic Society which stiffened its amateur performances of the choral repertoire with the theatre players. The Concert Society, however, used only the Imperial orchestra and chapel choir and so was an innovative step in the right direction.

The straitjacket of Tsar Nicolai I meant that the efforts of his predecessors, Alexander I and Catherine the Great, had been wasted and Russia was now lagging behind its counterparts to the west. As it was with Russia's railways, education system, social reform and international trade, so too with the structures of musical life. Theatre, however, was beginning to emerge from this period of reaction. French plays were

The Alexandrinsky Theatre in St. Petersburg, the city's Imperial theatre for drama where Ostrovsky's plays and later Modest Tchaikovsky's were produced.

34

Pyotr Ilyich, the young man about town in 1860.

especially fashionable, largely because the authorities tolerated its vaudeville style as being safe from any political intent. Most educated Russians in St Petersburg regarded French as their second language and it became a mark of their budding sophistication for the young men at the School of Jurisprudence to patronise it. The fare at the two Imperial theatres, the Alexandrinsky (in St Petersburg) and the Maly (in Moscow), was solidly presented and, until Alexander Ostrovsky's first play was mounted in 1853 in passably modern dress, was stuck in the production style prevalent when Nicholai came to the throne 30 years before. The one attempt in his reign at bringing a hint of naturalistic modernism to Tsarist taste, Nicholai Gogol's *The Government Inspector* (seen at the Alexandrinsky in 1836) had met with such official disapproval that Gogol put himself into voluntary exile for more than a decade. The liberal regime of Alexander II took some time to produce artistic change. Nonetheless, although St Petersburg was backward in comparison with Berlin, Vienna, Paris or London, it was the best Russia had to offer and many times more interesting than Tchaikovsky would have found in the Ural provinces from which he had come. It become immensely richer in 1859 with the foundation, under the inspiration of the brilliant young pianist Anton Rubinstein, of the Russian Musical Society (RMS), supported as patron by the new Tsar's aunt, the Grand Duchess Elena Pavlovna. The first concert, in which Rubinstein performed one of his own concertos, was given in November and from then on the musical life of the city was transformed. Within a decade the RMS had nurtured a school of composers and musicians of a quantity and standard it had never seen before.

In 1857 Pyotr's father and uncle tired of their shared domestic life and once again Ilya's family became self-contained. At 15 Sasha was deemed old enough to leave school and take over the running of the household and the care of her younger brothers: the twins, now seven, still at home under the care of Alexandra Petrova. At the same time, for some peculiar reason which must have made sense but which in retrospect was foolish in the extreme, Ilya entrusted all his savings to Natalya Yachmeneva, the widow of an engineering friend. Within six months she had lost all the money and despite years of litigation it was never recovered. More family readjustments suddenly became necessary. In the spring months of 1858 the house was relinquished; luxuries as they seemed then, such as Pyotr's private piano lessons, were curtailed and relatives were appealed to. His aunt Elisaveta Schobert (Alexandra's younger sister by ten years) took them in and Ilya started looking for a job once again, not an easy task for a man in his sixties already retired for more than five years. It is either a measure of the corruption in the Russian capital or of the respect with which Ilya Tchaikovsky was held by his peers that within a few months he was appointed Director of the Institute of Technology. The position was an important one, for Russia was at last making serious efforts to catch up with its imperial competitors in Europe and needed well-trained engineers to stimulate the country's long-delayed industrial revolution. In domestic terms it meant that the Tchaikovskies' normal standard of living could be restored (though with no capital base) and they could move into the spacious quarters that went with the post; so spacious in fact that the Schoberts abandoned their own flat and moved in too. Ilya was plainly happier when surrounded by as large a family as possible. Given the number of his own siblings this is hardly surprising.

1858 saw the start of Pyotr's last year at school and, in theory, of formal education. After the School of Jurisprudence it was not usual, as it would have been in Britain or America, to move on to university. Any further training, it was assumed, could be acquired during the course of employment in the legal system. No other career was to be seriously considered. It was, after all, what the choice of school had been about. The western system of educating first and specialising only at the end of the process has only recently found favour in Russia. Even throughout the Soviet era the elite picked their profession early and proceeded through dedicated schools. For those who had chosen well and had a vocation – or at least a competent interest – the system worked exceptionally well. However for those who found that they had taken the wrong path it meant that they left with few alternatives and had either to accept a life of employment in a profession to which they were unsuited or somehow start again.

Pyotr left school on 25 May 1859, two weeks or so after his nineteenth birthday. A few days were spent with his school friends walking in the country outside St Petersburg, perhaps the last formal gathering of his classmates which he afterwards always looked back to as a moment of particular emotional power. They had been together in constant contact for at least six years, after all, in some cases nearly a decade, and this interlude without the constriction of any institution was brief, for within three weeks Tchaikovsky was installed as a junior clerk at the Ministry of Justice.

In many ways there can have been few people less suited to the job. All his life he had been shambolically untidy and quite

Sasha Tchaikovsky and Lev Davidov
at their wedding in 1860.

incapable of remembering where he had set down papers
(sometimes he not only lost them – there is a story that he had
a habit of eating them as well). He had never shown any
interest in the legal system or its administration and like most
young men of his age what happened outside working hours
was far more interesting than his activities at the office.
Nonetheless most of his friends were in the same position and
however dull the routine it was far less arduous and demanding
than schoolwork. Tchaikovsky had a streak of self-discipline,
though, which always stood him in good stead. Even if his
emotional life was never entirely (or even at times moderately)
under control, he had the ability to force himself into a routine

and concentrate on the job in hand. He cannot have been completely hopeless as a civil servant for by the end of the following winter he had been promoted within the office to be a senior assistant. He was expected to work his way up the profession but, as would have been true if he had graduated from a military academy rather than a civil one, it was not expected of a young gentleman that he should spend all his time in service. Holidays were frequent and extended leave of absence was not difficult to obtain. Indeed it was a system which allowed members of the civil service to behave almost like a priesthood; one could be actively employed or not but once one was admitted to the ranks there was always a post available until a final resignation was submitted.

Away from work Tchaikovsky enjoyed his new-found freedom to the full. He was in a good place at a good time to do so. The new regime of Tsar Alexander II meant that the Russian capital felt like a freshly emancipated city. There was a sense of license very different from the stuffy puritanism of Germany, America or Victorian England, at least for men. While young upper and middle-class women were to be encountered and admired at home, parties, balls and at the theatre, they were still relatively unattainable physically outside marriage, even if Russia was more relaxed about sex than most western countries. Working-class women were regarded as easily available, however, and for high-spirited young men it was a simple matter to extend the enjoyment of good male company into sexual flirtation among themselves without any great risk of social exposure or professional opprobrium. It was little more than an extension of the adolescent exploration in which they had indulged at school. Some, like Apukhtin (whom Tchaikovsky saw nearly every day at this period), took it too far but even he became something of a society darling because of his homosexual outrageousness, which, combined with his wit and poetic brilliance made him a Wildean figure in the salons of St Petersburg. Tchaikovsky, by contrast, was naturally shy to the point of desperation and it usually took a few drinks to unlock his generous good humour in company that he did not already know intimately. Once over the worst, though – which seems to have been more frightening in anticipation than in reality – he relaxed into the popular and attractive young gallant that his acquaintances recognised. He thoroughly enjoyed the company and attention of young women, superficially relishing the flattery if they happened to fall in love with him, as at least two or three did in these years. Sex was safely out of the question, anyway, and his own uninvolved

Berlin in the middle of the 19th century. On his first visit Tchaikovsky thought it much inferior to St. Petersburg.

response kept any dangerous entanglements conveniently at bay for the time being.

Tchaikovsky was a young man about town from a respected family with money in his pocket for the first time, though, as he admitted to his sister Sasha, the debts soon began to mount faster than his income should have allowed. He could not resist the excitement of spending whatever came his way on pleasure. Exactly what these pleasures were, he did not elaborate. A picture of him from 1860 shows a good-looking, though not out-of-the-ordinary, youth, his short brown hair parted on the right (a style he changed within a few years) showing a wide forehead over deep-set eyes. There is a hint of a smile that suggests that holding the pose is rather a strain. He carries a shiny top hat in his right hand and his frock-coated suit looks warm and decently cut without being flashy. According to Fyodor Maslov, he would have liked to have dressed much more elegantly than his finances would allow. He was something of a social climber but the grand houses of the aristocracy were well beyond his reach.

His sister Sasha, by now a spectacularly lovely girl, was faring rather better. In 1860 she was getting ready to leave the Tchaikovsky household at the age of 18. She had been matched with Lev Davidov, a 23-year-old aristocrat from a family with a distinguished record of opposition to Nicholas I's regime. They were married in November and left St Petersburg for the family estates (for the management of which Lev was to be responsible) at Kamenka, 150 miles south-east of Kiev in the Dniepr valley of the Ukraine. It was to prove a good marriage for Sasha, in financial as well as personal terms, and while her departure from her brothers' immediate circle in the capital was felt hard, Pyotr was to find the estate at Kamenka a retreat from many of the difficulties which faced him over the next 30 years (as Pushkin had done a generation earlier). Sasha became pregnant within a few weeks of her marriage and the full extent of the duties the young couple had undertaken became clear in March 1861 when Alexander II decreed that hundreds of years of serfdom should end. For landed families like the Davydovs the changes were enormous, converting their bonded labourers into free men but doing little to alleviate the dependency of the peasantry. Russia, like Ireland, was to discover that land reform was a far more complicated and painful business than imperial decrees suggested.

By the spring of 1861 it had been nearly two years since Tchaikovsky had left school and, while he had diligently stuck to his desk in the Ministry of Justice, he was becoming less tolerant of the prospect of a lifetime there. The talent he had always shown at the piano and singing, his flair for improvisation and his facility for remembering passages of music he had heard only fleetingly, was beginning to mark him out from his comrades. At parties he was often called upon to

London's Crystal Palace (which burned down in 1936), the home of August Mann's popular concerts. Tchaikovsky heard, almost inevitably, massed choirs singing Handel here on his first visit to England.

Crystal Palace.

entertain and his usual shyness never manifested itself at the piano. It occurred to him for the first time that there might be more to his music than some dilettante performing in the drawing rooms of his friends. He was studying theory in more detail than before, given the opportunity by the classes the Russian Musical Society ran at the Mikhailovsky Palace, the Grand Duchess Elena's residence. Here, performance was tutored by Anton Rubinstein and theory by Nicholai Zaremba. It was not long before the subject of whether Tchaikovsky could find some way of switching professions was raised with the family. Interestingly it was his father, who had always been encouraging but had also insisted his son train for a more conventional career, that believed he could still find a way of moving into music if he wished. Tchaikovsky was not so sure. He wrote to Sasha,

'It would be splendid if that were so – but the point is this: if there is talent in me it is still most likely that it's impossible to develop by now. They've made an official out of me – and a bad one at that.'

The routine was clearly beginning to feel stifling but the chance of new adventures came in the summer when a friend of his father's, Vasily Pisarev, offered to take Pyotr around Europe with him in return for his language skills in French and German. They left in July with Berlin as the first destination. This first taste of 'abroad' Tchaikovsky found a huge disappointment.

'The town reminds me of St Petersburg but in a shabby way. The air is even heavier and more stinking and we did not see any water for the Spree is a parody of a river. It seems to me that everything the Germans have is a parody of other people.'

The music ('beneath criticism'), the dances ('queer'), the manners and especially the women (about whom he was devastatingly rude) all disagreed with him and after four days he was delighted to get to Hamburg, with its louche atmosphere and its sense of seafaring excitement, helped by the fact that he ran into two friends from school. Pisarev had work to do in Brussels and Antwerp and neither city impressed Tchaikovsky, who was far happier in Ostend where he could enjoy the sea and bathe in the summer heat. He crossed to England and arrived in London for the first time on 8 August 1861. He found it wet and gloomy ('interesting but it leaves a dark impression on one's soul') compared to the wide planned

The Palais Garnier, home of the Paris Opera, an altogether more uplifting experience than London.

avenues of St Petersburg. It was a filthy week to be there, though hearing massed voices sing the *Hallelujah Chorus* from *Messiah* at Crystal Palace (which he visited twice) was a highlight of the trip, outshining a recital by Adelina Patti and English food – plain and plentiful – which was much to his liking.

Paris was to be where they were to spend the longest time and Tchaikovsky adored the city on sight. Given his early indoctrination in all things French it is hardly surprising. He met up with friends from St Petersburg and went to the Normandy coast for a few days to stay with his cousin Lidiya, holidaying with her husband Olkhovsky (who was soon to become the Director of the Russian Royal Mint). These familiar contacts were a relief, for he was finding travel with Pisarev an increasing strain. Inevitably Tchaikovsky was spending too much; not only the money Pisarev offered to cover his expenses but the allowance from his father and a further loan from his travelling companion.

This did not immediately detract from the fun he was having in Paris, however, as he wrote back to his father (though prudently he leaves out any criticism of Pisarev at this stage),

'There [Paris] you may do anything you like, the only impossible thing is to be bored. We go to the theatre almost every day and we have been to the opera twice (*Trovatore* and *Les Huguenots*). Of course both the performances and the theatres themselves are much inferior to those in St Petersburg but the sets and ensembles are good...'

Finally he fell out with Pisarev sufficiently to return to Moscow on his own and to denigrate him to Sasha as vile and base. After three months abroad St Petersburg seemed more like home than ever. As he put it with wisdom beyond his years, to be really enjoyable travel 'needs complete freedom of action, sufficient money and some reasonable cause'.

Despite all this the trip had done much to mature Tchaikovsky, at least professionally. Once home he found the family circle contracting. His elder brother Nicholai had become a mining engineer like his father and Ippolit had joined the Navy. Tchaikovsky moved out of his father's apartment into rooms with friends of his own age and pushed ahead on two fronts simultaneously. Money and a new-found desire to make something of his creativity were the twin spurs. When he wrote to Sasha that in three years she might be hearing his opera he was only half joking. He had already had one composition printed and issued at Leibrock's music shop; a song in Italian called *Mezza Notte* for tenor and piano. For the first time the possibility of doing more was firming into a determination and his studies of thorough-bass were becoming serious. In order to achieve time to work on music and to enjoy the young buck's lifestyle he craved, however, he realised that he would need to earn more. With the diligence that had brought him through his schooldays he therefore set about trying to prove his worth at the Ministry of Justice. He was encouraged by the hope that he might earn promotion to be Clerk of Special Commissions, a post that carried with it a raise of 20 roubles and a less exacting schedule.

'Society life in Petersburg is at its height... So I am often out, although I do not go to the theatre as often as before. Two evenings in the week are taken up with study; on Friday I am either at Piccioli's or Bonne's, at home on Sundays while every Monday we play octets at someone's house...'

So determined was he to impress that he forsook his usual summer break in 1862 at the country retreat his father ran for his Institute of Technology students and stayed at his desk in St Petersburg. The sacrifice was alleviated, however, by the attractive presence of his 16-year-old brother-in-law, Alexei Davydov, who often visited Tchaikovsky's apartment with the twins, Anatoly and Modest (now 12) and stayed on occasion.

The separate apartment and the zest for work at the ministry did not last long, however. At the end of the summer Tchaikovsky found out that all his demonstration of enthusiasm had been in vain. He was not promoted and the prospect of an attendant rise in salary vanished with the job. It was the most important turning point in his life. The disappointment was huge for he had persuaded himself that he could tolerate life in the Ministry only as long as it brought him enough money to pay for his pleasures in the city, gave him a sense of belonging to his peer group of graduates from the School of Jurisprudence, and at the same time gave him enough free time to develop his musicianship in a dilettante way, as his idol Glinka had before him; studying seriously enough with Zaremba to allow the prospect of turning to music once his fortune and security had been established.

All this seemed to have been put in jeopardy by his sudden failure to move up the ministerial ladder, as he had hoped and worked for so hard, and it also put his increasing passion for music in perspective. Life in the Ministry no longer seemed the automatic guarantor of position and financial stability it had always promised to be. Tchaikovsky relinquished the rooms in Mokhovaya Street and moved back home with his father and the twins. But there was another complementary development. Nicholai Zaremba, exasperated by his pupil's facile approach, had long since told Tchaikovsky that he had more talent than he was using and his father Ilya, with his two daughters married and two sons established in secure careers, could afford to be more encouraging of Pyotr's ambitions. Now Zaremba was to be the first professor of theory when in September, the free classes at the Mikhailovsky Palace were transformed into Russia's first proper musical training centre. On 20 September 1862 Anton Rubinstein opened the St Petersburg Conservatoire and within a week Pyotr Tchaikovsky was enrolled. He did not relinquish his post at the Ministry of Justice immediately but his life was never to follow a conventional path again.

Chapter 3

The Plunge into Music

The influence of Zaremba on Tchaikovsky's decision to join the first group of students at the St Petersburg Conservatoire was crucial. It ensured that the young musician joined a group which was firmly westward looking in its taste, drawing its ideas about structure and harmony primarily from Germany, with the occasional glance to Italy, though thoroughly disapproving of the liberties of modern French composers like Berlioz. Had Tchaikovsky not been going to Zaremba for his theory lessons over the previous two years his composing mentality might have been quite different. In 1862, for the first time in Russian history, there was a choice for the musical enthusiast. Six months before the Conservatoire opened under Rubinstein and Zaremba, Tchaikovsky's old music master from the School of Jurisprudence, Gavriil Lomakin, launched a very different venture, the Free Music School. Lomakin's partner in this, and its main instigator, was the impoverished but impassioned Mily Balakirev, whom Tchaikovsky might have first seen playing his own music at one of the university concerts in 1856. Balakirev was vehemently opposed to the westernising tendencies that Rubinstein and Zaremba represented. Like Lomakin his roots lay in the music of the Russian orthodox church and he believed that Russia should be developing its own musical personality, free from the fashions of the west. Round this idea Balakirev grouped one man in particular who came from a very similar background to Tchaikovsky; a young army officer, Modest Mussorgsky. Under Balakirev and Lomakin's influence he developed a style that came to be the antithesis of Tchaikovsky's, raw in its harmony, often inelegant, but brilliant in inventing a progressive sound derived from the mediaeval character of Russia. With serfdom only then beginning to be weeded from the society there needed to be nothing synthetic about this nationalism as there was in countries like England, Norway and Poland where the indigenous traditions had almost been extinguished by the time composers like Vaughan

Anton Rubinstein (1829-1894), composer, pianist, founder of the St. Petersburg Conservatoire, Tchaikovsky's teacher and frequently severe critic.

Ilya Tchaikovsky in late middle
age, wearing the military
uniform to which his seniority
in Russian public service
entitled him.

Williams, Grieg and Szymanowski began their explorations.

A great deal has been made of the rivalry between the two St Petersburg institutions (the Conservatoire and the Free Music School) which was indeed intense at the beginning – they were, after all chasing few students and limited patronage. However, though their philosophies were different, they both acknowledged the power of the pioneering work of Glinka and their older contemporaries Dargomizhsky (composer of *The Stone Guest*, a Russian version of Don Giovanni which still holds a place in the repertoire) and Serov. Perhaps one of the reasons why the rivalry was so sharp was because the circle on which it fed was so small. Zaremba, Mussorgsky and even Tchaikovsky all studied the piano with Anton Herke and Nicholai Zaremba's brother Vladislav remained at home in the Ukraine where he became a collector of the country's folk material and a composer of choral works derived from it. In spite of Mussorgsky's subsequent pillorying of Zaremba's views on harmony, they were all steeped in the debate about the emergence of Russia as an influential musical nation. Tchaikovsky, like those enrolling at the Free Music School, was still an amateur with a passion and this was recognised as he entered the new Conservatoire. There were only two formal classes each week and though there was a great deal of studying to do at home, the music did not at first interfere too seriously with his work at the Ministry.

Tchaikovsky was changing on his own, however. Nights of flippant sex and drinking; the dandy lifestyle he had enjoyed so much two years before, had lost its attraction. With the help of his father and Zaremba he was now convinced that music could and should be his life. It required dedication, though, and the evenings at the theatre were curtailed. He still saw Apukhtin and Adamov for light relief but without the daily frequency that had been their habit. His hair began to grow – perhaps in imitation of Anton Rubinstein – and his clothes were less cared for. Counterpoint, taught rigorously by Zaremba who was a strict Lutheran, harmony and piano practice came to dominate his life.

At the Conservatoire new friends soon appeared, very different from the legal set he had grown up with. Foremost among them was Herman Laroche, later to become a particularly conservative critic who did not let his friendship get in the way of giving Tchaikovsky some stiff reviews. Each week they spent an evening together playing through four-handed versions of scores borrowed from the music shop, learning and dissecting the music of Schumann, Glinka,

Beethoven and Wagner (not to Tchaikovsky's taste then or ever) as well as lesser known figures popular at the time like Litolff and their own principal, Anton Rubinstein, a figure of European stature as a performer and composer, though his works now seem a little wooden in comparison with his contemporaries. Laroche had firm, though not always discerning, tastes and he was a useful influence on Tchaikovsky whose own experience of music had, until then, been superficial and mainly a matter of accidental discovery. Hearing major works, by composers of their own time as well as the classics, was becoming much easier, though, with access as Conservatoire students to Rubinstein's RMS concerts.

As the winter wore on Tchaikovsky found his dual life – official law by day and music by night – increasingly intolerable and by the spring of 1863 he had decided that, whatever the financial hardships, he had no real choice. He would have to devote himself full-time to music. He was well aware of the risks and his brother Nicholai made no secret of his opinion that to give up the security of a ministerial position was sheer folly. The timing could not have been worse. Yet again Ilya Tchaikovsky could not tolerate his employers and in the same month as his son resigned from the Ministry of Justice, he resigned after five years as Director of the Institute of Technology, by now too old to find any other job. Instead of having two decent incomes and a comfortable apartment, they now had rent to pay and no income. Pyotr, it seemed, had a lot of his father in him after all. To Ilya's great credit, once he was sure Pyotr was serious about his decision he never opposed it, as his son recognised,

'...never in a single word did he make me feel that he was dissatisfied with me. He inquired about my intentions and plans with nothing but the warmest interest and in every way gave his approval. I am very, very indebted to him.'

Sasha, on her estate in the Ukraine with her toddler, Tanya, took more persuading. Tchaikovsky pointed out at length that the decision was not as mad as it might have seemed. If music proved to be a cul-de-sac, his position was not irrevocable. Under the rules of Tsarist service once one was admitted to the government, one was admitted for life. Just as it was possible in the military to join the reserves in times of peace without losing rank or prestige, so in the civil service it was possible to leave and pursue other activities until there was a pressing need to be recalled. In many ways it was an inspired system, allowing

Sasha Tchaikovsky Davidova in her twenties.

many members of the intellectual and landed classes to follow independent lives while giving the state a permanent list of qualified and experienced officials who could take on the many temporary or part-time duties that the government occasionally required. Tchaikovsky wrote to Sasha (who had just given birth to her second daughter) with a rare tone of admonishment in April, a fortnight before his resignation became effective,

'From your letter to Father received today I see that you have no real interest in my position and that you look with distrust on the decisive step I have taken... It is impossible to work conscientiously along with my musical studies. I cannot receive a salary for nothing all my life... In consequence there remains only one possibility: to resign from service (the more so since I can always return to it). In a word, after long reflection I have decided to put myself on the reserve list, giving up my staff position and salary.'

He went on to reassure her that this did not mean that he was going to live off his father, whom they both knew was in no position to let him do so. His studies were now far enough advanced to allow him to teach the piano in his own right.

'I hope that next term I will find a post at the Conservatoire and I have already found a few private pupils... As I have completely renounced all social pleasures, elegant clothes, etc., my expenses have diminished considerably... When I finish the course at the Conservatoire I dream of coming to you for a whole year to write something big in peace and quiet... Lent, with its concerts, has tired me a good deal. I have been perpetually asked to accompany at different concerts. I appeared twice on the stages of the Bolshoi and Mariinsky Theatres. Once I was at a musical evening at the residence of the Grand Duchess Elena Pavlovna. I had the honour to attract her attention and talk to her and two days later I received an envelope with 20 roubles (not very Grand-ducal !) in it...'

The fact that Tchaikovsky was already considered proficient enough as a pianist to play professionally at the centre of Rubinstein's circle and in public says much about the speed of his progress. So good was he that when he returned to the Conservatoire for the autumn term (having spent an unsatisfactory summer apart from his own family and with Apukhtin's parents instead) he was able to give up his formal piano lessons with Herke and concentrate on Rubinstein's orchestration class. He was having lessons on the organ too (a good way to learn how to manipulate colour) and the flute, so that he could experience sitting in the orchestra – it was his flute teacher, Cesare Ciardi, that he had accompanied at the Grand Duchess's salon.

With all the enthusiasm of a late convert Tchaikovsky threw himself into the orchestral world that Rubinstein opened for him. As well as studying scores in the library he made himself indispensable to his teacher, assisting him as often as he could at rehearsals, playing timpani and flute in the orchestra and helping organise concerts. It was a thorough education in the music business.

As part of the class he was expected and delighted to watch the Russian Musical Society concert rehearsals and those at the Bolshoi. He was particularly fired in May 1863 by the premiere of Nicholai Serov's opera *Judith*. Although this has not held a permanent place in the repertoire, at the time it was the most successful opera by a Russian since Glinka's. For Serov himself, at 43, the triumph which greeted it (acknowledged by all except the cabal at the Free Music School like Balakirev, Cui and Mussorgsky who seemed determined to declare war on anything produced at the official theatre) was a turning point. He had taken the same route as Tchaikovsky, resigning from the Ministry of Justice twelve years before. It had been hard. Serov was treated as something of a joke by all except the Grand Duchess and his previous attempt at opera nearly a decade earlier had been a disaster. By 1863 he had alienated himself not only from Balakirev but from Rubinstein and all at the Conservatoire as well. *Judith*, however, sent him to the top of the musical profession, provided enough profits for him to marry one of the cast and paved the way two years later for *Rognyeda*, a folk opera which earned him a pension from the Tsar and launched the penchant in Russia for fairy-tale themes which Rimsky-Korsakov – who admired the work but as a new member of the Balakirev circle, did not dare to admit it – exploited so effectively later in the century.

For Tchaikovsky, Serov was the first composer of any stature other than Rubinstein that he had a chance to meet and talk to (intriguingly he met Dostoyevsky the same evening). Within weeks of resigning, Serov was living proof for him that, despite the pitfalls, it was possible to leave government service and succeed as a musician and *Judith*, whatever its lasting qualities, was a heady experience. It is possible that Tchaikovsky had also seen (even if he did not meet) Wagner, Serov's idol, when he came to conduct the Philharmonic Society earlier in the year. It was a profitable trip for Wagner, earning him 4000 Austrian thalers and allowing him the financial breathing space to work on *Die Meistersinger*.

Tchaikovsky soon took up where he had left off at school under Lomakin five years earlier, conducting rehearsals of the choir at the Conservatoire. It was useful experience and Rubinstein soon put him in front of the orchestra too. One wonders whether he was taught in the old school of conducting which, bizarrely, had the conductor facing the audience rather than the orchestra, a practice derived from the days 30 years earlier when the music had always been led from the first violin, who, of course needed to have the instrument facing out into the hall. Wagner, on his visit that February, was the first person in St Petersburg to turn to face the musicians he was directing, a practice which seems so obviously essential it is extraordinary that it took so long to be introduced. Either way Tchaikovsky found that his natural shyness, never a problem when playing the piano, reduced him to a state of appalling

Alexander Serov (1820-1871).

nerves when conducting, manifesting itself in the alarming sensation that his head was going to roll off his shoulders unless he held it on by the chin with his left hand. It made conducting a nightmare – and must have looked distinctly peculiar – so that once the demands of the Conservatoire were satisfied it was many years before he willingly stood in front of an orchestra again. Nonetheless throughout the academic year of 1863-64 Tchaikovsky continued to establish himself in the eyes of Rubinstein and Zaremba as a gifted and exceptionally hard-working student. The days of playing the fool with friends from the ministry were put well behind him. He was beginning to look more mature as well. As his hair grew he stopped parting it at the side and adopted the style that he kept until his fifties, with it swept directly back from his forehead. The beard, that he also kept from then on, began to sprout. Though a photograph from 1864 shows it was a bit undistinguished at first, it did much to dispel the image of prettiness which he had had until then.

For the summer of 1864 he was asked to stay at Trostinets, the country home of Prince Alexei Golitsyn, still in the Ukraine but 100 miles or so east of Sasha's estate at Kamenka. How much of this was a friendly favour to a music student too poor to travel anywhere else and how much a sexual invitation it is difficult to say. Whatever the motive, though, the result was thoroughly satisfactory. As their holiday exercise Rubinstein had set his class the task of writing an overture. With typical enthusiasm Tchaikovsky seized the opportunity of two months in the luxurious surroundings of the Golitsyn estate – where the young composer's name-day was celebrated with a carriage ride into the forest at night lit by flaming barrels of tar to a feast laid out for peasants and gentry alike – to tackle his first major orchestral score. During the course of the year he had written exercise movements for his teacher and apparently tried his hands at a dramatic overture on the theme of The Romans in the Coliseum, all of them now lost or destroyed, but he had not yet set up about writing anything with public performance in mind.

Tchaikovsky could have enjoyed the summer in style and turned out a respectable but diffident little piece using the Mendlessohnian orchestra to which Rubinstein expected his students to confine themselves. This would have underestimated not only his own talent but the fire to compose seriously that had been building up inside him for the best part of three years. Pyotr had learned a lot and now he was desperate to show what he could do. If possible he wanted to write something that was playable at the RMS as well as the Conservatoire. For a subject to be the thematic base of the concert overture he turned to Ostrovsky's drama *The Storm*, first staged five years before and one of the most trenchant pieces of Russian theatre between Gogol and Chekhov. The play juxtaposes a story of marital and social breakdown with the storm in nature. For a late Romantic young Russian emerging at a time of enormous social change it was a perfect subject. When he first saw it Tchaikovsky saw himself writing an opera but eventually half a century later it was Janáček who did that, in *Katya Kabanova*, and showed why his predecessor was right to consider it. The work that Tchaikovsky produced is not long, a little over ten minutes, but it is intense and from the brooding first notes, immediately interspersed by the crash of the breaking storm, his personality is apparent. There are fragments of all the characteristics that he made his own later, from pits of emotional strife to elegant waltz rhythms, and if the quality is not evenly high throughout it is still an accomplishment than any composer in Russia in 1864 would have been proud of. For a first attempt at writing for orchestra it is remarkable.

Tchaikovsky uses a sizeable orchestra, complete with full brass, cymbals and harp, well beyond the neat little band Rubinstein had in mind (given the forces he himself deployed in his *Ocean Symphony* it is surprising how strict he was with the students: perhaps it was just a matter of expecting them to walk before they ran). The work was strenuous and Tchaikovsky concentrated hard, working most of the day and emerging for the entertainments in the evening. Writing to Sasha he claimed to be 'living very quietly' and seeing only Golitsyn, clearly something of an exaggeration designed to assuage her disappointment that he had not visited Kamenka but maybe containing a hint of the truth.

Despite the perfect composing conditions at Trostinets, the effort of the composition left its mark and he fell ill when he returned to St Petersburg in September for the start of his third year at the Conservatoire. This meant that he was unable to deliver the score to Rubinstein in person and it fell to his friend Herman Laroche to present it for him. The storm that greeted it from Rubinstein was every bit as spectacular as the one Tchaikovsky had depicted in the overture and Laroche found himself on a Sunday morning receiving the tirade that Tchaikovsky should have endured. Rubinstein had plainly found his temper again by the time the composer reappeared in his class a few days later but there was clearly no question of the

Tchaikovsky in 1863, during his years at the St. Petersburg Conservatoire.

work finding a place in one of the Russian Music Society's concerts. The work did not appear until three years after Tchaikovsky's death, when it was published as Op. 76 by Belayev and now it is easy to hear how unfair Rubinstein was, not for the last time, about his most illustrious pupil's music.

The rebuff was enough to set back any more ambitious projects until a later date, though during the autumn and winter he completed a set of *Characteristic Dances* and worked on his first Piano Sonata. Despite the official disapproval of *The Storm*, however, Rubinstein was impressed enough by his progress to let him begin teaching harmony to the junior students, a gesture which, together with the private pupils and work as an accompanist, made him almost self-sufficient financially, which was more than could be said for his father. In the spring of 1865 the complicated Tchaikovsky family arrangements changed yet again. The twins, aged 15, had followed Pyotr to the School of Jurisprudence. Ilya, who always preferred an extended household, had taken in a widow, Elizaveta Alexandrova and he decided to marry for the third time. Oddly they did not spend much time together at first for while Ilya decided to spend the rest of the year with Zinaida and her family a thousand miles to the east, the new Mme Tchaikovskaya remained with her own family in St Petersburg. This left Tchaikovsky without a household and as soon as he and the twins had finished their respective terms they set out for the Ukraine and Sasha's house at Kamenka.

There he was immediately happy and settled, though it was soon clear that there was a painful complication. His sister-in-law, Vera Davidova, was firmly in love with him. It was a situation that over the next few years forced him to confront the issue of his own sexuality without giving rise to either suspicion or offence in the family. For Sasha, who was beginning to feel cut off and constricted in her life of motherhood and Ukrainian gentry duties, the arrival of her brothers was a great fillip. Apart from the situation with Vera the stay was idyllic and productive. Rubinstein had found a way to augment Tchaikovsky's earnings by commissioning him to translate for publication by Jurgenson the *General Treatise on Instrumentation* by F. A. Gevaert, issued in French the year before. One wonders too whether the teacher was motivated by the thought that such detailed reading might make Tchaikovsky avoid the bad habits he had displayed in *The Storm*. Even with this work Tchaikovsky found time to wander through the estate collecting the tunes he heard the Ukrainians singing (though only one enchanted him enough to use in his own work) and to begin another overture, on a smaller scale than the year before, which he laid aside after a while for completion the following winter.

Clearly, though, he had not been as industrious as he should have been and on 27 August, at the tail end of the holiday, he began both a string quartet and an Overture in F. With Modest he headed back to St Petersburg via Kiev (where they were bored by the sights and the rain). It was an unpleasant journey, devoid of decent food for two days because of a royal party which had eaten the country clean just before them, and a carriage ride which brought them close to disaster on mountain roads.

On 11 September 1865, the day after Tchaikovsky returned to the capital, Johann Strauss the Younger was conducting his orchestra at Pavlovsk, the extravagant country palace and park created for Tsar Paul I (later assassinated), nearly 20 miles from the city centre. On the programme Strauss included the *Characteristic Dances* Tchaikovsky had written that spring.

Alexander Ostrovsky (1823-1886), the finest Russian playwright of his generation and Tchaikovsky's first, though quickly disenchanted, librettist.

Nobody had thought to tell the composer, however, and even though it was his public début he was not there to hear the reception, having seen a poster for the concert too late to be able to reach Pavlovsk in time. Laroche was able to give him a good report but it must have been a disappointment. Quite how Strauss, one of the most popular musical figures in Europe, came to be in possession of the unpublished dances is unclear – perhaps Rubinstein passed them to him. With hindsight, given the wonderful dance music Tchaikovsky was to write himself, Strauss was the perfect person to introduce his music to the world.

The fact that Tchaikovsky missed the performance seemed typical of his fortunes as he began his last term at the Conservatoire. Money was shorter than ever and, with no family home to go to in the city any more, he moved from one unsatisfactory lodging to another before pitching up at his aunt's which was as damp and cold as any and a long walk from the Conservatoire. An uncomfortable eye complaint, probably a touch of conjunctivitis, was plaguing him and he made it worse by refusing to see the doctor, relying instead on patent lotions which clearly did nothing. He was grateful to his new stepmother, though, for dealing with his laundry and keeping an eye on the twins at school.

Even with the inconveniences, which included being without a piano because of the damp conditions in his aunt's apartment, composition proceeded steadily. The String Quartet movement (and possibly more, though there is no record of a complete work) was finished and played at a student concert in early November and the Overture in F, scored for a small orchestra at first, was ready the same month and performed at a similar event on 26th, with Tchaikovsky conducting at a concert for the first time. His thoughts were turning to what he should do after he left the Conservatoire at Christmas. He still had his private pupils but they were not a career. New regulations at the Ministry meant that he was now expected to give some kind of service to justify his continuation on the list, even in the reserves. Ilya, solid in support of his son until now but perhaps swayed by Zinaida's conventional view from the provinces, where he was living, urged Pyotr to think seriously about taking up the job again. Nonetheless he was regarded highly enough by his teachers for Anton Rubinstein's brother Nicholai to hold out the prospect of some work after graduation. But it meant leaving St Petersburg for Moscow, then considered very much second best as a city, though both in theory shared the title of the nation's capital. Nicholai Rubinstein was emulating his brother by setting up a

Johann Strauss II, the first person to conduct a public performance of a Tchaikovsky work. This poster was printed for his summer concert at Pavlovsk in 1865.

Conservatoire there and he needed staff, though there was not the financial backing needed to attract south musicians of the calibre of Serov. For Tchaikovsky too such a move away would be a serious wrench. He would have to tear himself away from the family that remained in town. He was finding some of his numerous female relations a bit of a strain but Anatoly and Modest were a different matter, for he was closer to them now than he had ever been.

Nothing was definite yet, however, and in the meantime there was the small matter of graduation and, in order to achieve it, an examination in public which included the composition and performance of a set work, the title of which was determined by Anton Rubinstein. In an uninspired move he settled on Schiller's *An die Freude (Ode to Joy)*, which forms the last movement of Beethoven's Ninth Symphony, as the compulsory text for an occasional cantata – a form often requested by official bodies in Russia which normally brought out the worst in its composer up to, and including, Prokofiev and Shostakovich. The Schiller *Ode* was guaranteed to strike panic into any young composer and for Tchaikovsky, now 25 and staking everything on making a success of his move into music, it was paralysing. There were less than two months between the performance of the *Overture in* F and that of the *Cantata* on 10 January 1866. There was also the problem of living quarters. The noise, discomfort and family distractions at his aunt's made concentration even harder than usual. In the end Apukhtin came to the rescue and lent him his flat while he was out of town for a few weeks.

The result of this combination of unfortunate subject and unsettled domestic arrangement was bad and Tchaikovsky knew it. After the disastrous premiere nobody had a good word for it. Herman Laroche tried to cheer him up by writing him a letter expressing great hope for the future and telling him the best was yet to come.

'In you I see the greatest – indeed the only – hope of our musical future. You know quite well I am no flatterer; I never hesitated for a moment to tell you that your *Romans in the Coliseum* was a wretched piece of trivia and that your *Storm* a museum of anti-musical curiosities. Besides, everything you have done so far... is in my opinion only preparatory, experimental school-work. Your own real creations may not appear for five years or so.'

Laroche was remarkably accurate in his assessment but that did not do much to ease the pain at the time. Cesar Cui, who had begun his vitriolic career as critic for the Vyedomosti newspaper, was devastating. Though the review was not published until April the misery it caused was worse than if had been seen at the time. After giving sympathetic record to the fact that Tchaikovsky's cantata was written to the worst of briefs, he went on,

'all the same if he had any gift then at least somewhere or other it would have broken through the fetters of the Conservatoire.'

Tchaikovsky had been frightened something of the sort would happen. The graduation performance was particularly important, not only for him but for the Conservatoire itself, presenting its first crop of fully qualified students to the musical establishment of the Imperial household. He was so appalled at the prospect he failed to turn up, even though attendance and questions on the work formed part of his final exam. Not surprisingly Anton Rubinstein was furious and threatened to withhold the diploma. However, his rages had the advantage that, although they were fierce, they tended to dissipate quickly, and in the end Tchaikovsky was given a reasonable final report and a silver medal. He was at last a proper musician, though not yet a very exalted one.

Tchaikovsky in 1864, now with a beard and the hair swept back from the forehead rather than parted to one side, a style he kept until it started to go grey after his marriage.

Chapter 4

No Money in Moscow

Despite the unpromising start to the year the appointment as teacher of theory at the new Moscow Conservatoire had been confirmed by Nicholai Rubinstein. With the fury of Anton and the ridicule of his chosen profession ringing in his ears the decision to move away from St Petersburg seemed much easier than it had a few months before and Tchaikovsky left within a week of the graduation concert. In Moscow Nicholai Rubinstein took it upon himself to look after his new member of staff and insisted that he buy himself some new clothes with his meagre

Living above the shop: the first premises of the Moscow Conservatoire, which gave Tchaikovsky his chance to earn a living from music.

Nicholai Rubinstein (1835-1881); five years older than Tchaikovsky, he proved to be a staunch and generous friend, without whom Tchaikovsky would probably have had to spend many more years as a government clerk.

salary. Those in which he had arrived were beneath the standards expected of even the rather makeshift new Conservatoire. Rubinstein also suggested that he live in the large house which he shared with several of the other staff and which housed the Conservatoire teaching quarters. Tchaikovsky's room was small and separated only by a thin partition from Nicholai's, which made him feel inhibited when he wanted to write either letters or music at night. Although he had always been a sociable sort he was not in the mood for carousing and his shyness made starting new friendships in a strange city difficult. Rubinstein succeeded in dragging him out now and again: to dinner with his impressive circle (one of which was Ostrovsky) or to attend the opera and the concerts he was conducting at the Moscow branch of the RMS which he conducted almost like shadow of his brother, who was six years older. Had he wanted to Tchaikovsky could have become one of Rubinstein's chaotic companions, playing cards and drinking into the early hours at the English Club. For the most part though, Tchaikovsky now preferred to keep a quieter routine; to find his feet gradually and settle back into composing after the trauma of the awful cantata. He thought about starting an opera but did not pursue the idea, claiming that he couldn't find a suitable libretto and that none of those Rubinstein supplied for him were good enough. Instead, during the rest of January and February 1865, he finished the orchestration of the second of the two overtures he had started the previous summer and presented it to both Rubinstein brothers, hoping that they would include it in the RMS concerts and that it would mend the damage done by the graduation performance. It did not. Neither regarded it as worth performing, a view shared by the director of the opera.

Perhaps realising the damage this double rejection would do to Tchaikovsky's confidence, Nicholai Rubinstein offered to include the other overture, in F, which had been heard at the student concert in November that the composer had conducted, in a programme for mid-March. The gesture paid off and Tchaikovsky re-orchestrated it thoroughly, incorporating more brass and fuller textures, rewriting and expanding several of its sections. His nervousness began to disappear and he started to build a rapport with his new students, most of them women. When the fresh version of the Overture in F was introduced the success was everything that the disappointments of the previous two months had not been. Rubinstein had been right to wait for a work of reasonable standard with which to introduce Tchaikovsky to the Moscow public. Apart from the *Characteristic Dances*, in a popular suburban venue, this was the first time his music had been heard in a professional setting. The players and the audience alike approved, and Tchaikovsky was given a moving ovation when he appeared for the post-concert party. It was enough to make him decide that Moscow was perhaps not such a bad place after all and that maybe he should conquer the feeling that his residency there was only temporary.

Equally significantly, the experience gave him the confidence to tackle a composition on a much grander scale than anything he had attempted in his student years. As soon as the Overture in F was delivered he started work on a symphony. Remarkably, unless the String Quartet of the previous autumn had consisted of more than the one part which has survived, only in the Piano

Sonata of the year before had he extended himself beyond a single movement.

Cui's review in April might well have been the blow which reversed this positive mood. From one of optimism and creativity he was plunged into self-doubt and a neurotic obsession that he would not live to finish the symphony. Given his inexperience in tackling a work of this size it would not have been surprising to anybody except Tchaikovsky that he found its composition a strain. His living conditions at Rubinstein's, with the combination of Conservatoire clatter during the day and his host's social life at night, did not make concentration easy. Tchaikovsky worked long into the night, sleeping badly, and put up with a fractured routine during the day. Money was desperately short, short enough to rule out another summer trip to Kamenka, and he even ended up sleeping rough one night in St Petersburg (though quite why is hard to know, given the number of friends he could have asked to stay with).

By the beginning of the summer of 1866 his nerves were beginning to take toll of his sanity. He withdrew into himself, shunning people when he could and concentrating harder than ever on the symphony, which he began scoring by the middle of June. His spirits had been lifted briefly in May with reports that Anton Rubinstein had conducted the Overture in F successfully in St Petersburg, underlining the fact that neither the ghastly cantata nor Cui's review of it had done any lasting damage. After the first elation, though, even this success seemed to increase the pressure he felt that the symphony had to be made to work.

After some deliberation the arrangements for the summer holidays were agreed, with Anatoly going to Sasha and Lev's in the Ukraine, Modest and Pyotr staying with Lev's family in a dacha outside St Petersburg within walking distance of Ilya and his wife and relatives. This was a sufficiently complicated tangle of relations to allow Tchaikovsky to maintain his independence, writing and walking most of the day and joining the rest in the evening before going back to work at night. Once again, though, this timetable proved too much and after a doctor had given the opinion that his neurosis was close to incurable, Tchaikovsky solved the problem simply enough by abandoning nocturnal composition.

Despite this action, the symphony remained unfinished at the end of August when it was time to return to his duties in Moscow. He made the mistake of showing the work in progress to Zaremba and Rubinstein on his way through St Petersburg. Never a pair to allow a former pupil to cut the apron strings, they both treated the piece as an unsatisfactory student exercise,

Hector Berlioz (1803-1869). He was a shadow of his former self by the time Tchaikovsky met him in his sixties.

disapproving of its material and, in Rubinstein's case, informing Tchaikovsky that on no account would it be heard at the RMS. The return to Moscow was a despondent one.

Once back, however, life in the other Rubinstein household was more encouraging. The Conservatoire, along with Rubinstein and Tchaikovsky, had moved out into a bigger building, giving at least a bit more space, even if there was still a sense of living over the shop. Nicholai Rubinstein, always more generous in his opinions than his brother, liked the symphony a good deal. He agreed to play the Scherzo at the Moscow RMS in December and followed by presenting it and the Adagio the following February 1866 in St Petersburg, a somewhat disjointed way of performing a symphony but one which at least made sure that the young composer was in the public eye. Better still he gave Tchaikovsky his first official commission, an Overture, taking the Danish and Russian national anthems as themes to mark the marriage and visit to Moscow of the new Tsarevich Alexander and Princess Dagmar of Denmark. Finding peace and quiet to write during the day was almost impossible in the Conservatoire so Tchaikovsky did most of the composition in the Great Britain, an inn with enough rooms to be sure of finding a bolt-hole. The *Overture* was also premiered in February, not in front of the Royal family as had been intended, partly it seems, because of rearrangement of the official visits but also because Tchaikovsky had adopted the minor key for the Russian anthem, a definite breach of protocol. Nonetheless the work, of which he was always fond, was well received and royal favour was expressed in the form of a pair of gold cuff-links which the impoverished composer promptly sold.

One far-reaching consequence of his lodging with Nicholai Rubinstein was the fact that it put him at the centre of Muscovite artistic society. He was soon on excellent terms with Ostrovsky, the playwright who had provided the inspiration for *The Storm*, and was introduced by the baritone Konstantin de Lazari to the Director of Repertoire at the Imperial Theatre, Vladimir Begichev and his wife Maria Shilovskaya. At the beginning of 1867 Ostrovsky needed some instrumental music for his new work, *Dmitri the Pretender and Vasily Shuisky*, and Tchaikovsky duly furnished an Introduction and Mazurka by the time the *Danish Overture* was premiered on 11 February. He had been discussing the possibility of collaborating with Ostrovsky on an opera for at least three months and the dramatist agreed to provide a libretto based on his verse drama set in the seventeenth century, *The Provincial Governor (Voyevoda)*, written two years before. He handed the first act to Tchaikovsky in March and the composer set to work straight away. In the meantime though, Rubinstein had continued his patronage by asking for a virtuoso piano piece for performance the following month (12 April) and Tchaikovsky returned to the favourite Ukrainian folksong he had used in his earlier student string quartet to use as the basis for a *Scherzo a la Russe*, a convenient bit of recycling given the short space of time in which he had to write and Rubinstein had to learn it. Perhaps because of his preoccupation with the Scherzo, or perhaps just because he was as hopeless as ever about keeping his things in order, Tchaikovsky succeeded in losing the libretto for The Voyevoda. In the days before photocopying, carbon or computer printers, there was no back-up copy and Tchaikovsky had to approach Russia's foremost dramatist and ask him to rewrite the work. Not surprisingly Ostrovsky was less than delighted to oblige. The young composer did not help by pestering him to finish, complaining that without the words he had nothing to work on. It is the familiar complaint of many composers who fail to understand that an author works just as hard at a script as a composer does at a score; the words do not merely tumble onto the page.

Ostrovsky grudgingly obliged in June but there was now a coolness in the relationship which hampered progress, though they never broke off the friendship completely. Equally, though, Ostrovsky did not hurry himself to provide the rest of the text, no doubt because he was working on his next play, produced the following year, *Enough Stupidity in Every Wise Man*, which probably summed up his opinion of Tchaikovsky at that moment. The composer spent a pleasant but impoverished summer with the twins and the Davidov family at Haapsalu in Estonia, having abandoned the original plan for Anatoly and himself to holiday in Finland when they ran out of money and nearly stranded themselves on the wrong side of the Gulf. His emotional life was complicated by constant proximity to Vera Davidova who was hopelessly, in all senses of the word, in love with him. All she received for her devotion however, was the dedication of the set of three piano pieces, *Souvenir de Hapsal*, that he wrote during the visit.

The opera's advance was fitful, partly because there was not enough text to set beyond the rewritten first act, partly because the size of the undertaking, especially writing in a sustained way for singers, was a new experience for him. In Haapsalu he raided and reorchestrated the *Characteristic Dances* that Strauss had conducted two years before, retitling them *Dances of the Hay*

Maidens for the purposes of the opera. Once back in Moscow at the end of the summer the slow progress made him peevish, as was clear when he wrote back to Anatoly,

'I have just returned from Ostrovsky... There is not much to do and I wander aimlessly all day through the Conservatoire and the town... Ostrovsky continues to deceive me. I read in the papers in Petersburg that he had finished the libretto but it is not true and it was with great difficulty that I got the first act out of him. At present I am busy arranging my room and am buying a large table which will encourage me to stay at home and write my opera.'

Ostrovsky had by now lost interest in the project entirely, however, and the composer was left to construct a libretto for himself as best he could. Despite these frustrations Tchaikovsky doggedly continued to work at *The Voyevoda* and the following few months turned out to be the most successful and rewarding he had yet known. They also marked his acceptance as a figure of real consequence in Russian musical life. The first achievement was the publication by Jurgenson in the Autumn of the *Scherzo a la Russe* and an *Impromptu* which Tchaikovsky had written several years before and had not intended to include but slipped in because it was copied into the same manuscript book. These became Op. 1.

In December Nicholai Rubinstein conducted the premiere of the revamped *Dances in Moscow* to great acclaim and Jurgenson offered to publish them too, though in piano duet form rather than full score. News of the success reached St Petersburg where Balakirev had recently taken over as conductor of the RMS concerts from Anton Rubinstein, a change which must have seemed breathtaking to the respective hostile supporters, since it was clear that there was at least something of a rapprochement between the Free Music School and the Conservatoire, represented by Lomakin and Zaremba respectively. Balakirev set about ousting the Mendelssohnian influences of the previous regime and bringing forward the music of his own circle of talented amateurs – notably Mussorgsky, Rimsky-Korsakov and Borodin – as well as established figures of nationalist inclination like Dargomizhsky. Rubinstein's withdrawal also gave Tchaikovsky his chance, though he was reluctant at first to believe it, writing to Anatoly,

'I had a letter from St Petersburg begging me to send them [the Dances] there but I answered that I will do so only if I get an official paper signed by the board of directors. Zaremba, via Rubinstein, told me I will get one. If so, then you will hear them. These mean individuals look down upon me too much; one has to spit at them to make them feel one's worth.'

Tchaikovsky duly received his piece of humble pie, in person from Balakirev, though it was in the end Liadov who conducted the *Dances* later in the season and at an Imperial theatre concert, not the RMS (in his apology Balakirev included the typical injunction, which was intended to be flattering, that Tchaikovsky was 'a mature artist worthy of severe criticism'). One of Balakirev's first initiatives on taking over the St Petersburg RMS was to invite Berlioz – the idol of those mid-century composers who valued the free spirit over musical orthodoxy – to conduct his works in Russia. Eight concerts were given in the two capitals, including music by Gluck and the last four Beethoven symphonies as well as the *Symphonie Fantastique* and *Harold in Italy*. In January 1867 Berlioz' visit gave Tchaikovsky his first opportunity to meet a fellow composer of indisputable world renown. He was asked to give the valedictory speech at the dinner in Berlioz' honour following his Moscow concerts, reflecting his status as the brightest young composing talent in the city but also, one suspects, as a result of his fluent French, learnt so well in his childhood. Berlioz, though only 64, was by then a shadow of his young self, broken by bad health and, psychologically, by the death of his much-loved son, Louis, in Cuba the previous summer.

Tchaikovsky's right to be seen in such company was emphasised the following month when at last the First Symphony, subtitled *Winter Daydreams*, was played complete for the first time on 15 February. He reported the event to Anatoly, also mentioning a further performance of the pieces which had now become something of a popular favourite:

'My symphony was a great success, especially the Adagio... On Monday a big concert is going to take place here, at the Bolshoi Theatre, in aid of the starving and I am to conduct my own *Dances*. I am certain that it will be awful as I am more and more convinced of my lack of capacity to do so. But I could not refuse the request. Besides it is an easy piece.'

It was this fact that saved him. The orchestra were able to ignore the composer in front of them, paralysed with fright and quite unable to give them a sensible cue. The experience was enough to make him refuse any further requests for nearly a decade. *The Voyevoda* was now going well, though, and he was able to report to Anatoly that he was in the process of orchestrating the third act and expected to have the work completed by the summer. This was lucky because the following months turned out to be hectic enough to have precluded too much concentrated composition. At Easter he visited St Petersburg, seeing his brothers and the Davidovs but more significantly becoming something of an associate member of the Balakirev circle which met weekly at Dargomizhsky's house, where the old pioneer was working on his last major work and masterpiece, *The Stone Guest*, a version of *Don Giovanni* (Mussorgsky used to act the part of Leporello in the initial try-outs of each scene). Sensing that Tchaikovsky was ripe for his brand of paternal artistic domination, Balakirev welcomed him into the fold, though there was a certain amount of distrust at first, as Rimsky-Korsakov remembered,

'He proved a pleasing and sympathetic man to talk with, one who knew how to be simple of manner and always speak with evident sincerity and heartiness. The evening of our first meeting he played for us, at Balakirev's request, the first movement of his Symphony in G minor; it proved quite to our liking and our former opinion of him changed and gave way to a more sympathetic one, although Tchaikovsky's Conservatoire training still constituted a considerable barrier between him and us.'

Alexander Dargomyzhsky (1813-1869), as the composer of *The Stone Guest*, considered the model for the younger generation, especially Mussorgsky and Rimsky-Korsakov.

For Tchaikovsky, however, the approval he found in this formerly hostile gathering contrasted clearly with the rejection his music had received from his old Conservatoire mentors. Although his residences in Moscow meant that he was never part of the suffocating clique of Balakirev's kuchka, or 'mighty handful', he was always a welcome visitor.

A barrier of a different sort was becoming evident during his trip home and this one caused him considerable anguish. It was all too clear now that the affection which Vera Davidova had made plain to him in Haapsalu the previous summer (and to which he had responded in a way which he regarded as playful and brotherly but which she read as encouragement) had blossomed into a full-blown expectation of marriage. This caused him great pain, not just because he had to admit to himself – and, with more difficulty, to his sister Sasha – that he was not in love with Vera and never would be, but because he was coming to realise that he could not commit himself passionately and emotionally in the manner that women expected of him. While relationships were bound by the rules of nineteenth-century civil conduct between the sexes of the same

67

class, he had no difficulty with, indeed relished, the company of women. But when they expected more of him he could not deliver it. After his visit to St Petersburg he wrote to Sasha in April,

'I am well aware how this should have ended but what would you have me do if I feel that I would have come to hate her if the question of our culminating our relations in marriage had become serious?'

He managed the situation with Vera tolerably well, though she interpreted his necessary escape as coldness, and he avoided the humiliating row which could easily have soured relations with his sister's family, something that he was desperate not to do. Another summer in their vicinity was out of the question, however, and he was quick to see the possibility of rescue in a proposed trip abroad with four male friends, two of them extremely useful professionally if he wanted to see *The Voyevoda* on stage. His companions were Konstantin de Lazari, the singer, Vladimir Begichev, the Imperial Theatre's 40-year-old head of repertoire, and his step-son Vladimir Shilovsky, aged 16. The ostensible reason for inviting Tchaikovsky was to give the consumptive Shilovsky music lessons on the trip, which was being undertaken partly for fun and partly to consult Parisian doctors on the prospects for Shilovsky's condition. He was, of course, just the sort of sickly, slightly effeminate adolescent that Tchaikovsky found attractive and made a welcome contrast to the nubile womanhood of 20-year-old Vera.

The party spent the second week of June in Berlin – where the sensitive composer was badly distressed by the sight of a snake eating whole a live rabbit at the zoo – and then made their way as quickly as possible to Paris, abandoning the plan to tour Europe because of Shilovsky's increasingly urgent need to see the doctors his step-father had in mind. His condition precluded too much sightseeing, which suited Tchaikovsky who had seen most of them before on his previous visit. Instead the four of them settled down to a regular routine of getting up late, some gentle work (the heat, Tchaikovsky reported back to Sasha was 'indescribable') and in the evening a visit to the theatre or the Opera Comique. The Parisian standards impressed him more than they had done seven years earlier and he could now appreciate the subtleties of the French ensemble acting tradition. However he regretted refusing his sister's invitation to the Ukraine, passed up for the chance of being entertained at rich people's expense, about which he felt embarrassed, and soon felt homesick as he always did and always would whenever he left Russia for any length of time. *The Voyevoda* was fully scored when he returned and he had the chance to play it through to Begichev whose support was vital if he wanted to have the work produced.

The approval must have been enthusiastic because back in Moscow, when the score was delivered to the Director of the Bolshoi, Stepan Gedeonov, he announced that he would give the premiere in October – those were the days when opera houses did not need three years and innumerable planning meetings in order to mount a new work. Even by those standards, though, six weeks was an ambitious schedule to learn and produce a new work by a composer who had never written an opera before. No doubt the fact that Ostrovsky was credited with the libretto (even though only the first act was actually his work) and that the papers had been discussing the project a year before, gave Gedeonov reason to believe that he was not dealing with a total risk. The singers soon confirmed his judgement and when Tchaikovsky was summoned to talk to him at the end of September he found the chorus already in rehearsal and the opening date confirmed for the end of October. Even to him this seemed to place impossible rehearsal demands on the theatre, especially since there was an Italian company occupying the building at the same time, and he wrote to Gedeonov threatening to withhold rights to the work unless it was postponed until the end of the year. The Director reluctantly agreed and the premiere was rescheduled for January.

In the meantime Tchaikovsky had no intention of sitting around waiting. He quickly penned the *Valse Caprice*, Op. 4 for piano in October and in late September, the day before he went to see Gedeonov, he started explorations of another large scale form which he had not tried so far, the symphonic poem. It is likely that the fashion for Liszt – of whom Tchaikovsky was only a lukewarm admirer – which was raging in the Balakirev circle, made the form attractive and it had the advantage of allowing him more experience of a full orchestral score without having to contemplate the labour involved in a formal symphony. *Fatum*, as the work was portentously called, occupied him until December when rehearsals for *The Voyevoda* moved into their final phase.

Chapter 5

Theatre Apprentice

The Italian opera company that were inhabiting the Bolshoi during the autumn of 1868 had one great crowd-pulling asset: the leading Belgian soprano Désirée Artôt. She was the daughter of the Professor of French horn at the Brussels Conservatoire and studied singing with the great Pauline Garcia Viardot (sister of Maria Malibran, favourite of Berlioz and Meyerbeer and the first person to introduce the songs of Glinka and Dargomizhsky to the west). At 22 she sang for Queen Victoria in London and the next year joined the Paris Opera for a season before devoting herself to the Italian repertoire and embarking on her extraordinary peripatetic career in which she became famous throughout Europe. By the time she reached Moscow she had a reputation in Italy, at Covent Garden in London, in Berlin and Brussels, though she had turned her back on Paris.

Tchaikovsky was captivated by Artôt in a way that, try as he might, he had never managed to be by Vera Davidova. Artôt was 32, vivacious, a fine musician and, after ten years of performing, a confident international star. They had met briefly at supper after a benefit performance earlier in the year but it was only when Anton Rubinstein insisted that Tchaikovsky accompany him to visit her that he came properly under her spell (or so he asserted; it is quite possible, given the chronology of Rubinstein's visit, that Tchaikovsky had initiated the affair himself earlier). Thereafter he saw as much of her as he could, calling on her almost every evening. Her power as an actress enraptured him, especially when he saw her as Desdemona in Rossini's version of *Otello*. He set about writing music for her, some choruses and recitatives for insertion into Auber's *Domino Noir* and, more personally, a *Romance in F* for solo piano, which Rubinstein included in an RMS concert on 20 December, at which he also conducted yet another performance of the *Dances of the Hay Maidens*. By then Tchaikovsky was admitting to his brothers that he was 'very, very much' in love.

Désirée Artôt (1835-1907), the Belgian mezzo-soprano photographed at about the time Tchaikovsky was pursuing his brief infatuation with her.

The affair was a delicious topic of conversation in the artistic world of Moscow. There were echoes of the way Artôt's teacher, Viardot, had captured the heart of Turgenev 20 years before, so much so that he moved to Paris with her and set up an extraordinary ménage à trois with Louis Viardot, her equally literary husband. It was precisely this threat of losing Tchaikovsky to the demi-monde of operatic touring which made the Rubinstein brothers, Laroche, Kashkin and the rest of his friends to urge Tchaikovsky not to marry Artôt. They were aided and abetted by Artôt's formidable mother who travelled everywhere with her. He was well aware that he did not want to subordinate his own composing abilities to the more fragile career of a prima donna and the feeling that he could not live without her was tempered by 'calm reason' which 'bids me stop and think'.

In the event the matter was decided for him with a brutality which can have done nothing for either his faith in women or his self-confidence as a lover of them. Soon after the performance of the *Romance in F* the Italian company left the Bolshoi for Warsaw, ironically to make way for Tchaikovsky's opera. Artôt clearly felt that at 32, and with her mother in close attendance, she needed a husband in a hurry and one who would share her disjointed life. The handsome but very Russian young composer was not, after all, likely to fulfil her requirements and so in Warsaw she engaged herself to one of the other members of the company, the Spanish baritone Manuel Padilla y Ramos (whom, Tchaikovsky complained, she had ridiculed in Moscow). The news was broken to Tchaikovsky by Nicholai Rubinstein and de Lazari. The jilted lover went white and left the room but otherwise outwardly coped with considerable aplomb, within a month describing the turn of events as 'droll'. Work was a real consolation, however, and he was discovering again, as he had in his first months as a student at the St Petersburg Conservatoire, that the freedom to compose was more important to him than the freedom to pursue his emotional and social life.

The Voyevoda, meanwhile, was ready for production and was first performed on 11 February 1869. Tchaikovsky described the success as brilliant and noted that he had been called to the curtain fifteen times, though how much of that was enthusiasm for his new work and how much admiration for the principal singer, Alexandra Menshikova, for whom the premiere was a benefit performance, became clear over the following days. In reality the staging, cobbled together from bits of scenery in stock, the inexperience of the conductor, Eduard Merten, and the incomplete mastery of the new idiom by the composer meant that public and press reaction was guarded at best.

Hermann Laroche (1845-1904). As a music critic he was fierce, as a man he was a trial to friends but his early faith in Tchaikovsky was important to his development.

Hermann Laroche, until that point the closest of Tchaikovsky's musical friends, showed the lack of tact for which Rimsky-Korsakov later damned him and attacked the work in print, accusing it of being insufficiently Russian and imbued with German convention. Tchaikovsky was furious and they barely spoke to each other for the next two years. In fact the work was a clear indication of Tchaikovsky's emerging style (though he later destroyed the score it has been reconstructed from surviving parts), blending a hint of the nationalism championed by Balakirev and his cohorts with the more cosmopolitan world of Rubinstein and his own predilection for French and Italian music. Despite the mutterings of contemporary critics with narrow views, it has been precisely this grafting of western European elegance onto a firm root of Russian temperament which has made his international reputation so enduringly popular. This blend was shown again in the set of 50 folksong arrangements Tchaikovsky set for Jurgenson over the following year.

A fortnight after *The Voyevoda* was produced Rubinstein conducted the first performance of *Fatum*, the symphonic poem written the previous autumn. It was greeted with politeness, except by Laroche, which was enough to encourage Tchaikovsky to send the score to Balakirev, to whom he dedicated it. Balakirev reacted fast, including it in the RMS programme at the end of the month, but he could not work up any enthusiasm for it and in his usual paternalistic way wasted no time in telling the composer that he basically agreed with Laroche (though not with his analysis of the faults) and compared *Fatum* unfavourably with *Les Préludes* by Liszt which he had included in the same concert. Tchaikovsky quickly came to agree that it was not his best work and promised to dedicate a better piece to him before long.

The surprisingly mild reaction to the failure of his latest orchestral work was perhaps due not only to maturing self-criticism but to his preoccupation with a second opera which he had begun in January while *The Voyevoda* was being prepared and he was recovering from his abandonment by Désirée Artôt. This time he avoided any criticism that he was being insufficiently Russian by picking a ready-made libretto of a story which had no Russian content whatever, that of *Undine*, the water nymph who, jilted by her lover knight, transforms herself into a fountain after his death. It also gave him the chance to work through his disappointment of the Artôt affair by dealing with a saga of ruined love.

Vera and her family had come to Moscow and she was quick to try to capitalise on the failure of the marriage plans, so much

Mily Balakirev (1837-1910), composer, religious zealot and inveterate purveyor of advice, sometimes helpful, sometimes decidedly not.

so that the thought of spending another summer among the Davidovs made Tchaikovsky contemplate avoiding going to Kamenka, which he had already missed for several years. The opera progressed fast, however, and by April 1869, as he neared completion of the first act, he extracted a promise from Gedeonov to stage *Undine* in November if he had it finished by the start of the season in September. Tchaikovsky was as good as his word, and the summer at Kamenka allowed him to work on it uninterrupted by city commitments, with the result that he had the score in Begichev's hands by the middle of August. Nothing then happened until October when, according to the original promise, the work should have been in rehearsal. Gedeonov apologised, pleading that there was no longer room in the programme of the season for another new work, though half-heartedly promising to find a slot for it if events permitted. In reality *Undine* had been rejected and it never was produced at the Bolshoi or anywhere else. For Tchaikovsky, after the failure of *Fatum* and the lukewarm reception of *The Voyevoda*, *Undine* marked a low point, perhaps the lowest point, in his reputation as a composer. At 29 he was in danger of losing the status of the brightest hope of Moscow music which he had enjoyed for nearly five years.

Ironically the one person who now seemed to believe in his talent as a composer was the one whose circle had been so scathing about his Conservatoire manners in the past: Balakirev. He had spent much of August in Moscow, staying in the same house as Tchaikovsky, to the latter's pleasure but mounting irritation too. Balakirev was an intense and overbearing personality who was only really happy with a friendship when he had near-total control of the creative output. As a composer, he was more conservative than the radical nationalism he preached but when he criticised a work the remarks were usually astute, though not as infallible as he believed. Still, his relentless energy and demand for creative attention was a bulwark against official indifference for Tchaikovsky in the summer of 1869. Balakirev was in some distress himself, having been ejected by the Grand Duchess Elena from the conductorship of the St Petersburg RMS in an argument over the experimental repertoire that formed his programmes: so much harder to listen to than the safe fare served up by Anton Rubinstein. The replacement was the young Czech composer Eduard Napravnik, who had also taken over the musical directorship of the Mariinsky Theatre that year and was, by all accounts, an excellent conductor with far more authority over the orchestra than Balakirev. To Napravnik's credit the programmes he presented turned out to be just as controversial as his predecessor's.

Balakirev's great contribution that summer, not only to Tchaikovsky but to posterity, was to suggest a programme for an extended Overture on the theme of *Romeo and Juliet*. He laid out the musical plot, suggested a beginning (together with a long description of how he had approached the subject of *King Lear* several years before) and bullied Tchaikovsky to fulfil his promise to write something better for him than *Fatum*. In limbo because of the non-production of *Undine*, it was just the sort of pressure Tchaikovsky needed and by October he reported back to Balakirev in St Petersburg that the work was going well, was fully sketched and that it only needed another six weeks' work. He acknowledged his debt to Balakirev, telling him that the scheme both for the action and the key modulations were taken from his plan. Tchaikovsky finished the work by the end of November and promptly began work on his first set of six original songs – published in the spring as Op.6 – perhaps as a reaction to both Désirée and Vera arriving back in Moscow at much the same time. However he was not yet ready for the sort of barrage of detailed analysis he knew Balakirev and his circle would subject the work to and so declined to show Rimsky-Korsakov and Balakirev the score of *Romeo and Juliet* when they visited him a few weeks later.

When they did receive it the Mighty Handful were delighted, though as expected, not uncritical. 'Now there are six', their mentor Vladimir Stasov exclaimed after Balakirev had played it through to them on the piano. Their enthusiasm was not matched by the public when Nicholai Rubinstein conducted the premiere in Moscow on 16 March 1870. Two weeks later there was the same indifference to a group of excerpts from *Undine*, programmed to chivvy the board of the Bolshoi but without effect, and to the first St Petersburg performance of *Fatum*. Tchaikovsky had reason to be despondent and to feel that the musical world had lost interest in his work. After rejecting various new opera projects he had intended to devote himself to setting *The Oprichnik*, a tragedy by Ivan Lazhechnikov who had died in his seventies a few months before. Unusually for Tchaikovsky he could barely summon up interest himself. The best he could manage were two little pieces for solo piano, *Valse Scherzo* and *Capriccio*.

Shortly after his 30th birthday, with the Conservatoire term and therefore his teaching obligations over, he left for St Petersburg where he was told that *Undine* had been formally dropped by Gedeonov, and from there made his way to Paris to stay with the ailing Vladimir Shilovsky, who was ill but not as ill as he seemed (he eventually died only a few months before Tchaikovsky).

There was barely time in Paris to take in a couple of visits to the theatre before Tchaikovsky removed Shilovsky to the tedious but restorative atmosphere of Bad Soden, an uninspiring little spa just outside Frankfurt. He quickly became bored, relieved by a few day trips to surrounding towns like Wiesbaden where he met up with Nicholai Rubinstein, busy losing money at roulette in the town's casino. There was ample time for writing but instead of furthering the next opera or a new symphonic project he settled down to revise *Romeo and Juliet*, convinced now that some of the reaction to it had been the fault of the work rather than a personal slight.

Bad Soden, the appropriately named little spa town near Frankfurt where Tchaikovsky spent dull weeks just before the Franco-Prussian war broke out in 1870.

This calm interlude was shattered in the first weeks of July by the outbreak of the Franco-Prussian war. With the rest of the visitors Shilovsky and Tchaikovsky made a hasty exit from the Rhineland, though they did not make directly for Russia. Instead they headed south to Switzerland and the majestic landscape around Interlaken. Tchaikovsky was thrilled by what he saw, though he found the invasion of English ramblers trying, and took to walking in the mountains with unbounded energy in the six weeks he was there. The experience was lost on Shilovsky but Tchaikovsky's own state of mind and physical fitness was immensely improved by the time in the Alps. He left for home with the new version of *Romeo and Juliet* unscored but complete in all its other details. On the way back he stopped in Munich and then joined his brother Nicholai for a few days in Vienna, his first visit to the city that was at that time the centre of the musical world.

Although it was to be two years before the revised *Fantasy Overture*, as he termed *Romeo and Juliet*, was performed he was right to take the time and care that he did over the score (he returned to it again for yet more revisions ten years later). Balakirev's judgement was sound in declaring that it was Tchaikovsky's best work to date and the security of its structure, its vitality and the confidence with which the changes of mood are handled shows how far his work had matured since the *Winter Daydreams* Symphony. Equally importantly, it was the first work that showed Tchaikovsky's genius for flowing melody, the effortless lyricism which has guaranteed him lasting fame but which has also earned him the derision of musical snobs. If it was to be a few years yet before Russia was completely convinced of his talent, *Romeo and Juliet* brought him quick recognition abroad when, in 1871, it became his first orchestral score to be published, not by Jurgenson but by the Berlin firm of Bote and Bock.

Within months of completing the revised *Fantasy Overture* Tchaikovsky embarked on a work that re-established his credentials among his musical friends. This was not an orchestral or vocal work, at which he was now reasonably proficient, but his *First String Quartet*, a form which he had dallied with as a student but had never taken to a publishable conclusion. Composing the piece gave him little difficulty and it was done with the immediate purpose of presenting something in public that would score a success, without it becoming involved in the more intrigue-prone worlds of the Imperial theatres or Russian Music Society. It formed the centrepiece of a concert of his own works that Tchaikovsky promoted on 28 March 1871. Around it were placed songs, sung by the young mezzo Elizaveta Lavrovskaya, a duet from *The Voyevoda*, two of his Op. 9 piano pieces played by Nicholai Rubinstein and a new trio, *Nature and Love*, written for two sopranos, alto and piano. But it was the Quartet, led by Ferdinand Laub, and including the Ukrainian folksong he had heard at Kamenka two years before as its *Andante Cantabile*, that stole the evening, prompting Turgenev to congratulate him afterwards, an endorsement by one of the great men of Russian cultural life which was as influential as it was gratifying.

The success was deserved not only because of its inherent quality but because Tchaikovsky was proving to be a pioneer, for no Russian composer except Anton Rubinstein (who had by that stage written six) had produced a quartet of major significance. The *Andante Cantabile* is a truly inspired piece of lyric writing, deeply rooted in its ethnic origin but at the same time set and developed with a deftness that in its very gentle restraint makes it one of the most successful miniatures of late romantic expression. The movement soon became detached from its Quartet context, appearing in versions for violin and piano and cello and string orchestra: the first of Tchaikovsky's pieces to become a popular lollipop.

As far as he was concerned, however, the String Quartet was not the major project of the year. He had returned to the opera, *The Oprichnik*, he had started in the early months of 1870, though at first with little more enthusiasm than before. Once the concert was out of the way, the prospect of spending the

Ivan Turgenev (1818-1883), the doyen of Russian letters, whose friendship with Pauline Viardot made him an inevitable point of contact for his countrymen in Paris. Tchaikovsky was deeply proud of the pleasure Turgenev took in his music.

first half of the summer at Kamenka was close and his own spirits had revived, however, the first act moved more fluently. At Kamenka he now had a small apartment to himself, where he could work away from the distractions of the extended family which gathered there. When not composing, the childish side of his nature was given full rein and he threw himself into projects and games with his nephews and nieces that were so elaborate that they included a ballet – written, choreographed, designed and produced by Tchaikovsky – that became the basis for *Swan Lake* four years later.

Leaving Kamenka in July 1871 he also had to leave work on *The Oprichnik*, with only the first act complete, to write a harmony textbook – largely to help himself take his theory classes without having to invent the dull exercises on the Conservatoire blackboard afresh for each lesson – which Jurgenson was to publish in the autumn. His route back to Moscow took him via the country houses of his friends the Kondratyevs and of Vladimir Shilovsky, to whom he entrusted the job of writing some orchestral interludes for the opera. Once back in Moscow in the second week of September he took the long-awaited step to total independence of renting a flat of his own: it had only three rooms but was a great improvement on his quarters with Rubinstein for the previous six years. From the service of his colleague Ferdinand Laub he took Mikhail Sofronov as his servant to look after his domestic requirements, a move that confirmed his own emancipation from impoverished young composer to recognised musician and Conservatoire professor of several years standing with an income now in excess of 2000 roubles per annum, three quarters of which came from his teaching.

In theory the move should have made the writing of *The Oprichnik* easier but in fact the opera trundled along as slowly as it had the previous spring and though he set himself a deadline of the following spring, 1872, it was becoming something of a chore. He felt a break from Russia might give him a jolt and, apologising to Sasha for not joining her family for Christmas and joining in the celebrations over the safe delivery

The Place Messéna in Nice, even its temperate winter was not enough to soothe Tchaikovsky's homesickness in 1872.

258 Nice. Place Masséna, Terrasse du Grand Café Pomel

of her first son, he absented himself from the Conservatoire for a month and joined the consumptive Shilovsky who was wintering in Nice in the grand setting of the Place Messena, where the colonnades open out into the avenue of gardens that run through the city centre. Tchaikovsky travelled via Berlin and Paris, his first post-war visits. His reaction to being abroad and away from familiar surroundings was, as always, mixed, as he wrote to Anatoly,

'It seems queer to be transferred out of the deep Russian winter to a place where you don't need to wear a coat, where oranges grow, roses and lilac bloom and all the trees are bright green... I must tell you something strange. I waited for the day of my departure with such intense impatience that towards the end I lost sleep over it. But already on the day I started I was enveloped in severe homesickness which did not leave during all my journey and still has not left in this glorious countryside.'

The rain soon spoiled even the outdoor pleasures and he took a circuitous route back to Russia through northern Italy (including Venice) and Vienna, arriving in Moscow at the beginning of February 1872.

Once back at home the opera progressed at a manageable rate, satisfactory enough for him to be able to find time to compose (at a fee of 750 roubles which he was in no position to ignore) a Cantata for the bicentenary of Peter the Great, which was due to be performed in June. The fee was memorable but the music he delivered for it merely proved once again that commemorative cantatas were to Russian music what festival oratorio was to English: a diet of unseasoned stodge. Before that *The Oprichnik* was completed and despatched on 17 May to the theatre board in St Petersburg, though he remained only half confident that it would prove acceptable after the catastrophe of *Undine's* rejection. Despite this fear, another fee of 200 roubles for the premiere of the new version of *Romeo and Juliet* meant that there were signs that his future was not as bleak as it had seemed a year before. The Overture was played at the RMS where Balakirev, who was about to disappear from everybody's life for nearly a decade of religious retreat, was no longer the leading light: evidence that Tchaikovsky's reputation was now general and established.

On 12 June he left Moscow (his servant Mikhail being replaced for the duration of the holidays by his younger brother Alexei) to repeat the round of visits of the year before. He saw, though probably did not hear much of, since it was held in public gardens, the premiere of his *Peter the Great Cantata* and he missed its rather more conventional second performance at the Bolshoi later in the month. He seems to have shared the general view that it was not an omission about which to be too upset. The summer holidays took him for a month to Kamenka and then, with Modest, to Nizy, the Kondratyevs' estate, before a short visit to Shilovsky. It was on the last leg of the return journey that he nearly suffered the disaster of losing his luggage, including his money, papers and newest work. Only the intervention of an honest postmaster, curiously also named Tchaikovsky, saved the day.

The new piece showed a streak of determination in the composer Tchaikovsky's character which came out in his creative work but was so often missing in his personal life. After the criticisms of the previous few years he was aware that the compositions that were not only working to the advantage of his reputation but also earning him an increasing amount of money were those which either had a strong and satisfying romantic musical structure or took inspiration from national song: *Romeo and Juliet* and the String Quartet. With this in mind he set about writing another Symphony when he arrived at Kamenka in the middle of June 1872, aiming to construct a piece which combined theoretical strength and thematic accessibility. This firmness of purpose is immediately apparent in the opening *Andante sostenuto-Allegro vivo*, one of his least sentimental and most Brahmsian symphonic movements – though he was, as so often, dissatisfied with the work after a while and revised it thoroughly in 1880 before the publication of the full score, cutting a large chunk out of the finale and radically revising the first and third movements; only the slow movement, ironically rescued from the wedding march in the ill-fated *Undine*, survived without more than adjustments to the scoring. Since he was in the Ukraine, it was from there that the folksong elements were mostly taken, eventually earning the symphony the subtitle *Little Russian*, the somewhat patronising nickname for that country current in Moscow and St Petersburg circles at the time.

Tchaikovsky's confidence was further enhanced when he arrived back in Moscow by a huge raise in salary of 800 roubles from the Conservatoire (his starting pay only seven years before had been a mere 500 roubles a year), enough to make a bigger flat affordable. On top of this he was also beginning to earn a reasonable amount from musical journalism, though he resented the time both activities took away from his composition. Nonetheless the Second Symphony was finished by the end of

Eduard Napravnik (1839-1916), the Czech composer and conductor who established the Mariinsky Theatre in St. Petersburg as one of the world's great opera houses. As well as Tchaikovsky's works he also took charge of the premiere of Mussorgsky's *Boris Godunov*.

Lensky's original design for Ostrovsky's play *The Snow Maiden*, for which Tchaikovsky composed the incidental music.

November 1872 and he confidently reported to Modest, 'I think this is my best creation, so far as perfection of form is concerned – a quality which I have hitherto failed to achieve.'

It was an opinion shared by the remaining members of the Balakirev circle (minus Balakirev) when he showed them the score over Christmas at Rimsky-Korsakov's house. At much the same time he was told that *The Oprichnik* had at last been accepted for production and that it would be published by Bessel. Rather to his surprise and discomfort the opera approval committee asked Tchaikovsky to be present at the meeting at which its fate was to be decided but after it ended well he felt sufficiently relaxed to spend a rare week staying with his father. Tchaikovsky was exhausted by the effort of finishing the symphony and suffered one of his bouts of nervous reaction, though even he admitted there was nothing actually wrong with him. Nonetheless the routine of composing kept him going and before the end of 1872 he had also written a little *Serenade* for chamber orchestra, in celebration of Nicholai Rubinstein's name-day, and embarked on his next set of six songs, published the following year as Op. 16. Adroitly Tchaikovsky dedicated the new symphony to his champions at the Russian Music Society's Moscow branch and earned himself 300 roubles for the favour. Originally the premiere was scheduled for the end of January 1873 but official mourning for the Society's founding patron, Grand Duchess Elena, meant that it was postponed for a fortnight.

A month later, on 7 March, Eduard Napravnik conducted the *Second Symphony* in St Petersburg, where it was received more favourably than any of Tchaikovsky's works so far. Nicholai Rubinstein was enthralled enough to programme it again in April – when Tchaikovsky was called to take a bow after every movement – and again in May. Only Mussorgsky and Cui dissented from the general approval, but Cui gave everybody filthy reviews and for Mussorgsky there was too much of a tinge of the west in Tchaikovsky's music for it to meet his strict standards of nationalist fervour, even though the introductory theme of the last movement presages his own *Pictures at an Exhibition*.

Correspondence with another member of that circle, Vladimir Stasov, during the winter of 1872-73 led him to consider a trio of subjects for his next project: *Taras Bulba* by Gogol (another subject later treated brilliantly by Janáček), Sir Walter Scott's *Ivanhoe* and, returning to Shakespeare, *The Tempest*. Before any of these could take more definite shape, however, his old friend and unenthusiastic librettist Ostrovsky asked him for some music for his new drama *The Snow Maiden*, with an enticing fee of 350 roubles attached.

The commission, in March, left only three weeks to complete a score which went well beyond the normal requirements of instrumental music and, coming at a particularly busy moment in the Conservatoire year, it taxed Tchaikovsky to the full, forcing him to break his usual habit and compose in the evenings. Matters were not helped when he cut his hand badly, hampering his ability to write. The romantic fairy story of *The Snow Maiden* did not have much impact when it was performed by the company of the Maly Theatre at the Bolshoi (to accommodate the large orchestra required by the score) in May 1873. However, the music was conducted later in the season at a concert by Rubinstein, so Tchaikovsky's work was by no means wasted (though Cui was foul about it as usual) and for a long time Tchaikovsky toyed with the idea of expanding the already substantial score into an opera. When Rimsky-Korsakov pipped

Vladimir Stasov (1824-1906), the intellectual driving force behind 'the mighty handful' of St Petersburg composers. It was Stassov who suggested *The Tempest* as subject matter for Tchaikovsky.

him to it nine years later Tchaikovsky was unreasonably upset and it became the one real rift in their otherwise long and close friendship.

After a year of impressive compositional achievement he decided that he deserved the summer off and resolved to travel at his own expense (which meant chasing his publishers for some advances) and on his own for the first time. At the beginning of June 1873 he set out, but did not make immediately for, the west, instead calling first at Kamenka for a few days largely spent recovering from a cold. From there he went to Dresden before heading, via Cologne, for Switzerland, which he wanted to explore more thoroughly after his revelatory time there three years before. In July he crossed the Alps into Italy but, he reported to his father, found the heat too much to bear and retreated to Paris, by far his favourite foreign destination, before making his way back to Russia and Shilovsky's estate at Ussovo.

Shilovsky himself was in Moscow which meant that Tchaikovsky found the services of the house were entirely at his disposal for two weeks. He was immediately and blissfully happy and the combination of the peace and the landscape rejuvenated his composing zeal which had lain dormant all summer. In between walks through the woods and across the steppe he sketched all the basic material for a Symphonic Fantasy on *The Tempest* in eleven days, a feat which, when allied to the speed at which he had produced *The Snow Maiden*, proved, not least to himself, that his compositional facility was improving out of all recognition from only three years before. The spell was broken, though, when Shilovsky returned, for Tchaikovsky was becoming more and more irritated by the shallowness of his mildly consumptive young friend. During the autumn of 1873 back in Moscow this irritation increased, partly because so many of his other close companions, like his host during three summers at Nizy, Kondratyev, were away from the city for one reason or another and he found himself rather thrown on Shilovsky's company more than he found comfortable. Tchaikovsky took refuge in work, orchestrating *The Tempest* and writing a dozen piano works, the *Six Pieces* Op. 19 and the *Six Pieces on a Single Theme*, Op.21. Once again a major orchestral work scored an impressive success when Rubinstein introduced it to Moscow on 19 December. Like the Second Symphony, *The Tempest* was immediately popular enough to be repeated there and in St Petersburg (where Stasov was thrilled by the results of his suggestion) during 1874.

Tchaikovsky's extraordinary new ability to compose at

breakneck speed, even when embroiled in demanding teaching commitments, was demonstrated early in the New Year when he began and finished his *Second String Quartet* in the month of January 1874. His boast to Modest that he wrote it 'almost at one sitting' was hyperbole but not by far. The Quartet came to him with a fluency that even he was rarely to enjoy. Nonetheless it is a strange work, at times personal and romantic at others almost an elegant exercise, reflecting perhaps the contradictions he was beginning to feel in his own life. At the professional level his position as he neared the still young age of thirty-three seemed stable and assured. He had become a recognised and admired ornament of society in Moscow and St Petersburg, familiar not only to musical colleagues but to the Royal family and the rest of the social elite as well.

In personal terms, though, life was becoming more complicated. The discontents of the autumn had deeper roots that mere irritation with Shilovsky. Many of his friends were now getting married and starting families, or reaching a period in their professions where they had less time to spare for single acquaintances. His homosexual friends caused an acute problem too, for Tchaikovsky was at heart deeply conventional and he had no wish to join the group like Apukhtin who openly flouted social acceptability and relished the reputation that came with such declarations. What was regarded as playful behaviour in boys and young men about town was looked at very differently in men over thirty. Tchaikovsky's position was increasingly difficult, caught between his desire to be loved and respected and his physical needs for sex without women. The interludes of loneliness and with them depression, apathy and misanthropic disgust were becoming more pronounced and prolonged. Seventy years later Benjamin Britten was to suffer something of the same agonies. Coming to terms with nature, when there was a deep rift between the desire and the self image, was not yet the torture it was to become but the stirrings of disquiet were starting to show.

In the meantime the *Second Quartet* was given a private performance at Nicholai Rubinstein's house two weeks after it was completed, to everybody's pleasure except Anton Rubinstein who – never able to shake off the master–pupil relationship – lost no time in telling Tchaikovsky that he did not consider it a proper work of chamber music. The public heard the quartet a month later and, although it did not achieve the popularity of the *First Quartet*, greeted it with enthusiasm.

Chapter 6

Average Opera, Great Ballet

During the winter and early spring of 1874, Tchaikovsky spent a longer period with his father than he had for many years when he travelled to St Petersburg for the rehearsals of *The Oprichnik*, which had been scheduled to open in April. Napravnik was to conduct the production and he had contacted Tchaikovsky before Christmas to discuss casting arrangements and some cuts he wished to make. Originally the composer, anxious to see the opera on stage without any more delay, agreed with the proposals. However as rehearsals progressed he became increasingly annoyed by Napravnik's attitude, which was rather more radical than he had bargained for. If the conductor irritated him, however, the opera itself now irritated him even more, its combination of Meyerbeer and Russian nationalism sitting uneasily together. By the rehearsals for acts three and four he had retreated from the theatre in disgust – he never did learn to like the work. *The Oprichnik* reached the stage of the Mariinsky Theatre on 24 April 1874 and was more successful with the public than it was with its composer, who damned it as being without style or inspiration and predicted – entirely inaccurately – that it would close after six performances. In fact, though Cui hated it too, as ever, it turned out to be more appreciated by contemporary audiences than *The Voyevoda*.

Tchaikovsky, thoroughly disenchanted, promptly left St Petersburg for Venice, the excuse being that he had to review the first staging at La Scala, Milan of Glinka's *A Life for the Tsar* (which had in fact been postponed by the time he reached Italy). In reality, despite the public warmth for his most recent works, *The Tempest*, the *Second String Quartet* and *The Oprichnik*, he was glad for once to leave Russia, though the dissatisfaction was with himself. Italy was not much of an improvement, however. Venice was unseasonably cold and the dank narrow passages, the dirt-encrusted palaces and the press of foreign tourists depressed him. If he had to spend more than five days

Henry Litolff (1818-1891), French composer, now underrated but in his own time a figure whose music Tchaikovsky admired.

there, he wrote back to Modest, he was likely to hang himself. He only stayed a day and a half, enough to find out that *A Life for the Tsar* had been rescheduled for May, before he headed for Naples and some warm weather. In Rome he paused to look at the sights, marvelling at the Coliseum and the Vatican but, he wrote to Anatoly, speaking to no-one except servants and railway guards. As it turned out the weather was no better in Naples – 'without the sun it is nothing', he wrote, though Pompeii fascinated him and made up for much of the rest. Beset with loneliness and homesickness he cut short his stay, abandoned the plan to see Glinka's opera in Milan (which he had heard was dreadful) and made his way home, the only consolation being the few hours he spent discovering Florence.

In Moscow once again he pulled himself together, glad to be home and secure in his routine. The Conservatoire was still in session so he fulfilled his obligations then turned his attention back to opera. Against his expectations he found that the St Petersburg public had not shared his disgust at *The Oprichnik*. Indeed it had been such a success that it was to be produced at theatres in Odessa and Kiev as well during the following season. While he could not share the enthusiasm, the news was still encouraging and he decided to compose another score as fast as he could. Instead of searching for a new subject, however, he took, for him, the unusual step of entering a competition. Two years before, the Grand Duchess Elena had suggested that the RMS commission an opera for production at the Mariinsky with a top prize of 1,500 roubles. Now that she was dead the Society's committee decided that the competition would make a suitable memorial for her and chose Gogol's *Vakula the Smith*, adapted by Yakov Polonsky, as the set text (though deviations from the selected libretto were allowed).

Tchaikovsky knew that he would have to write the opera faster than his other two if he was to have a hope of having it finished by the time the new term started at the Conservatoire in September but believed he had a certain amount of leeway, since he thought the deadline for submission to the judges was January the following year. He decided that his lawyer friend Nicholai Kondratyev's house at Nizy, near Sumy, 150 miles east of Kiev, would be a suitable bolt-hole for the summer with a regular routine of early rising, mineral water and games of bezique. Kondratyev and his wife were unfailingly optimistic in their outlook, a quality which always lifted Tchaikovsky's spirits and encouraged him to work.

After six weeks *Vakula* was sketched, ready for orchestration, which he tackled at Shilovsky's house before returning to

Hans von Bülow (1830-1894). There seem to have been few important events in his musical lifetime in which von Bülow was not involved. For Tchaikovsky, however, his greatest service was introducing the First Piano Concerto to America.

Moscow. He arrived there in September confident that he had written, in record time, his best opera so far and that he had more than made up for the horrors of *The Oprichnik*. When he delivered the score, however, he had a shock. It turned out that the deadline was not January, as he had thought, but 13 August. He had missed it by a good three weeks. Determined that, whatever the results of the competition, *Vakula the Smith* should reach the stage, Tchaikovsky wrote to the Chief Producer at the Mariinsky asking him to withdraw the entry. This letter was shown to Napravnik and Grand Duke Konstantin, the dedicatee of the *Second String Quartet*, who were both furious at what they regarded as a flagrant attempt to circumvent the rules and push Tchaikovsky's claims separately from the competition. It would have left any other composer who did win in the impossible position of having the winning opera staged alongside another on the same text by a more famous contemporary composer. Tchaikovsky had to apologise and explain himself. The matter did not end there, however. The judges included Laroche, Rimsky-Korsakov, Napravnik and Nicholai Rubinstein, the last of whom conducted the Overture (half-heartedly disguised as an *Overture to an Unfinished Opera*) at an RMS concert in December 1874, many months before the judgement was meant to be made. It is inconceivable that his best friends would not have recognised his style, even if they had not noticed that the motto which headed the copyist's score was in his handwriting.

Meanwhile in October Tchaikovsky proceeded with the vocal score and wrote to Modest that he 'would like to start a Piano Concerto but somehow I have neither ideas nor inspiration.' As was becoming usual, though, once he settled down to compose the work progressed fast, though all through November he complained to his brothers that it was proving hard, that he was stuck and that he was feeling sluggish. As with *Vakula*, he completed the main work in seven weeks, a period that also saw the Kiev performances of *The Oprichnik* and the St Petersburg premiere of *The Tempest*.

Tchaikovsky was sure enough of the material to play through the concerto in progress to a group of friends gathered at a party on Christmas Eve, a group of colleagues that included three Nicholais: Hubert, Kashkin and Rubinstein. The result was traumatic and totally unexpected. Rubinstein reacted, not like the trusted supporter he had been for nearly a decade, but like his antagonistic brother. He denounced the concerto as impossible, technically and structurally, vulgar and derivative (the last a particularly sensitive accusation since Laroche had

Sergei Taneyev (1856-1915), perhaps the most brilliant of Tchaikovsky's pupils whether as pianist, composer or Director of the Moscow Conservatoire.

just published an article arguing that Tchaikovsky had little musical personality that could not be traced to Litolff, Schumann, Glinka and Berlioz). Tchaikovsky, shocked, retired to an upstairs room where Rubinstein, realising that he had over-reacted, sought him out but instead of apologising repeated his criticisms and loftily offered to perform the work if comprehensive revision were made according to his prescription. Tchaikovsky refused and told him that the concerto would be performed and published as it stood.

In belligerent and depressed mood he spent January 1875 orchestrating it and penning a little work of miserable protest, the *Melancholy Serenade* for violin and orchestra. Despite the unsettling reaction of his erstwhile friends, Tchaikovsky was right to press on, for, with his usual enterprise he was entering a new phase, eschewing the lures of nationalistic opera and instead embarking on his first works for solo instrument and orchestra. It was a process which moved him from the relative backwater of Russian music – however talented the close-knit group of which he was part – into the mainstream of European art. His *First Quartet* and *Romeo and Juliet* had begun the process, establishing for him at least a foothold in Germany (where Liszt, the kingmaker of European musical taste, had professed himself impressed) but the First Piano Concerto was to establish him on an altogether more exalted level.

It has always been assumed that Rubinstein most objected to the violent opening which – on piano alone – must have sounded impossibly bombastic on first hearing. With the orchestral fanfares, though, and the brilliant dexterity of the piano writing later in the first movement, the magnificence and freshness of the work becomes clear and launched two generations of Russian piano concertos from Glazunov via Rachmaninov to Prokofiev, pulling in Gershwin along the way and linking their era with the earlier tradition of Anton Rubinstein. The sheer originality of much of the writing, combining as only Tchaikovsky did, the occasional elegant French turn of phrase of the sort pioneered by the Scots-Alsatian composer Henry Litolff, the attempted structural cohesion of Schumann and wild Russian passages (especially in the final Allegro) that could have been by Mussorgsky, was more apparent to foreign audiences at first than to the Moscow elite. With this he contrasted the bravura with moments of daring simplicity and tenderness. It is one of his most optimistic and accomplished works, despite Tchaikovsky's professed sense of isolation in the months that he composed it, and deserves more critical favour than it received either from its first listeners or from modern writers, sated with its popularity and too many performances by indifferent musicians.

Nurturing the hurt, Tchaikovsky did not begin any new major work in the first few months of 1875, preferring instead to concentrate on definite commissions and clearing the decks. As well as the *Melancholy Serenade* for Leopold Auer, he orchestrated the Concerto, dedicating it at first to his young pupil Sergei Taneyev who was becoming a fine soloist as well as an exceptionally gifted composer. Tchaikovsky found the opportunity for more theoretical writing, this time on harmony appropriate in Russian church music, some reviewing, his teaching and the composition of songs (of which he wrote 18 before the spring, for his two main publishers Bessel and Jurgenson). In an inspired move, perhaps prompted by some favourable comments about him written in the German press, Tchaikovsky sent the score of the Piano Concerto to Litolff's pupil Hans von Bülow, perhaps the most influential performing musician in Germany after Liszt. Unlike Nicholai Rubinstein, von Bülow was delighted with the work (and the dedication, which Tchaikovsky had now switched to him from the less powerful though more faithful Taneyev) and wrote back in June 1875 offering to give the first performance, not in Europe, but on his tour of America the following autumn.

This reply, together with a commission of 800 roubles for a ballet from the Imperial theatres, despatched Tchaikovsky to the Ukraine for the summer in a much more cheerful frame of mind. At Shilovsky's house he was joined by Prince Golitsyn and in the three weeks spent there Tchaikovsky alternated between steaming in the new bath house and walking with his friends, while he began work on the project he had set himself for the holidays, a third symphony. Much of the thematic work was complete by the time he left Shilovsky for his usual ten days with Kondratyev and by the time he arrived at Sasha's house there were only final revisions and a touch of orchestration left to be done, so that he could record that he finished the symphony on 13 August 1875.

Astonishingly he moved straight on to the commissioned ballet, to be called *Swan Lake* with a scenario by Shilovsky's step-father, Vladimir Begichev. At the end of the summer break many of the preliminary thoughts were already on paper. Back in Moscow the autumn proved to be exceptionally busy and *Swan Lake* progressed in fits and starts. News came from Boston that von Bülow had given the world premiere of the Piano Concerto on 25 October where, despite the player's irritation with the semi-professional orchestra (the Boston Symphony was not to be formed for another six years) it was an instant success. As the tour went on, so did the public's approval. On several occasions von Bülow was called back to repeat movements. A few days later the jury on the Grand Duchess Elena's memorial opera competition met to award the 1,500 rouble prize for the setting of *Vakula the Smith*. To nobody's very great surprise (except, possibly, the winning composer's, considering the machinations he had gone through to get it) Tchaikovsky was chosen. The jury covered itself from allegations of misconduct by making it clear that it was the best by such a distance that nobody else's score came near to meeting the aspirations of the competition.

In November the *Piano Concerto* was given its Russian premiere in St Petersburg by Gustav Kross with Napravnik conducting. Tchaikovsky was disgusted with the performance and returned to Moscow, only to be just as disappointed with the *Third Symphony*, which Rubinstein was rehearsing for its first performance on the 19th. He was right to feel that it was not up to the standard of the *Second Symphony* or, indeed, *Romeo and Juliet*. Despite the spontaneity with which it had been composed, the feeling that emerged was one of caution and constraint, as though he had been so careful to be strict with himself about symphonic correctness that he had forgotten the need for first-rate melodic material. It remains the least-played and recorded of all his symphonies. Even when not at his best, though, Tchaikovsky was as competent as anybody writing in Russia at that time and his music was never less than enjoyable.

Far more satisfying was the performance in Moscow at the RMS on 3 December 1875 of the *Piano Concerto*. The satisfaction was due on several counts. Firstly it received a far better prepared and comprehensible performance than it had in St Petersburg. Secondly it revealed the full talent and musicality of Sergei Taneyev, aged only 19, who had been working on the part with Tchaikovsky's help all autumn; and thirdly it marked a *volte face* by Nicholai Rubinstein who, having abused the piece so intemperately almost exactly a year before, now conducted it with great skill and appreciation. By the end of the decade he had learned the concerto and performed it himself, as Tchaikovsky had hoped he would all along.

As well as mending the fences with Rubinstein, December also saw Tchaikovsky enjoy a brief but riotous friendship with Camille Saint-Saëns, who was giving concerts of his own ten days after the Tchaikovsky concerto was heard. Oddly the two seemed to regard the warmth they generated as an isolated moment for both of them. Tchaikovsky showed no inclination to

The original 1875 production of Bizet's *Carmen*, which Tchaikovsky saw a few months after its premiere.

visit the French composer in Paris only a few weeks later and the relationship never amounted to anything other than polite cordiality again.

With a flurry of performances in the autumn months of 1875, *Swan Lake* progressing slowly but steadily, *Vakula the Smith* safely scheduled for performance the following season and 1,500 roubles from the prize in his pocket, Tchaikovsky concluded that he could spend Christmas away from Moscow. He did not even have to feel guilty about neglecting the family. Sasha, pregnant yet again, and Lev were staying with the children in Geneva and Modest wanted to travel abroad for the first time. Like his elder brother, Modest had decided that he could no longer face life in the civil service but the job he had decided to take instead was just as hard. He was to become tutor to a boy of seven, Nicholai Konradi, who was deaf-mute, a job which entailed learning some special needs skills at an institute in Lyon. There was time before he needed to arrive, however, and so the brothers embarked on their trip west together. After Berlin and Geneva, they inevitably gravitated to Paris, where they saw *Carmen*, in its first season still charged with emotion from Bizet's death within days of the opening. For Tchaikovsky seeing an opera as musically and dramatically relevant to modern life was an experience he was never to forget. Immediately the only result was a musical nod towards the work in the little *Dance Espagnole* he included in *Swan Lake* but the real legacy was his occasional abandonment of the nationalistic style he had championed until then in opera and the more international approach to the genre adopted instead in *Evgeny Onegin* and *The Queen of Spades*.

Two days later, still overwhelmed by the revelation that *Carmen* represented, Tchaikovsky left for St Petersburg, where Napravnik was due to conduct the *Third Symphony* a couple of weeks later, a performance which proved to be more convincing than Rubinstein's in Moscow, thus neatly reversing the experience with the *Piano Concerto* before Christmas. There, between social calls on family and old friends like Laroche and Apukhtin (and even Cui, despite the frightful notices he kept publishing) he worked on a new String Quartet, dedicated to the memory of Ferdinand Laub, the violinist who had led the premiere of the *Second Quartet* – also played for the first time in St Petersburg that winter – only two years before.

As with the previous works, Tchaikovsky finished the *Third Quartet* in a matter of weeks, and by 4 April 1876 it had been heard four times, in private performances at Rubinstein's and at an evening for the Grand Duke Konstantin – another important ally with whom Tchaikovsky had now made peace after the *Vakula the Smith* affair – then in two concerts for the public, where it proved to be his most successful chamber piece yet. Pleased with the reaction to all his music (he had heard from von Bülow that the *First Quartet* was also being greeted warmly in America and from Edward Dannreuther that the *Piano Concerto* had gone down well at London's Crystal Palace), he decided to relax during the spring. His idea of relaxing, however, was to finish *Swan Lake* and produce a piano piece for publication each month in *Novelliste* magazine. The piano set was to be called *The Seasons* and was to run for a year, a neat way of keeping his name before the general public unable to attend city concerts without too much hard work. He finally completed *Swan Lake* on 24 April 1876 and delivered it to the theatre, where the ballet staff were delighted. So much had happened in his life since he had started the work that Tchaikovsky himself had virtually lost interest in it, though he was always pleased when other people were pleased. The process of choreography was completely foreign to him, though he had always enjoyed mimicking dancers, and he found it faintly absurd at first acquaintance.

Once *Swan Lake* was out of his hands he headed west once again, determined not to begin a major project until he had decided on a suitable subject for a new opera. Although he was cheerful enough for the moment, his physical health had been uncertain during the winter. He had suffered recurring bouts of a feverish complaint, which he was advised required a cure with the waters of Vichy. However, he did not reach Vichy until July after a series of unsatisfactory stays at Nizy, Kamenka and Vienna and one happy period with Modest in Lyon.

When he did finally arrive in Vichy the admittedly beneficial effect on his stomach complaints of a sober routine and constant glasses of mineral water was offset by the fact that he loathed the place and was appalled by all he saw. He wrote to Anatoly,

A page from Tchaikovsky's autograph of the piano score of *Swan Lake*.

'Everything has conspired to make my stay here impossible. Up at five to get a bath, crowds round the well where one drinks the waters, the worldly way of life, the absolute lack of natural, beautiful

94

surroundings and complete loneliness – which poisons all my life. I feel so melancholy that I doubt if I shall stay the whole course. For all I know I shall run away to Lyon.'

This was precisely what he did do, absenting himself after eleven of the prescribed 21 days and returning to Modest for a far happier, though emotionally complicated, fortnight in the south of France. After this, he had to be in Bayreuth to continue his sporadic journalistic career with a review of the first complete cycle of Wagner's *Ring*. There he found half of the Russian musical establishment gathered: among them Laroche, who had taken to drink, Cui, who inevitably quarrelled with Laroche, and Nicholai Rubinstein, with whom Tchaikovsky shared rooms. Wagner himself refused to see him when he called (but then he was refusing to see most people) but Liszt was pleased to meet him at last and was flatteringly kind. The music of the *Ring* baffled and irritated Tchaikovsky. *Das Rheingold* he characterised as an 'impossible medley' with 'extremely beautiful and extraordinary details'. By the time the end of *Gotterdämmerung* came he felt he had been let out of prison, the wonderful passages obscured by the fact that he found the whole thing excruciatingly boring – a reaction that many of those who are not committed Wagnerphiles have shared over the years.

Arriving back in the Ukraine for two weeks with Sasha before the end of the summer holidays was a great relief. There he found two of his other brothers, Ippolit and Anatoly, as well as his father and step-mother. He was once again secure in the bosom of his family. As Sasha busied herself with charitable works among the local poor, Tchaikovsky found something of the atmosphere he had so loved as a boy in the Urals, a delight he found too playing with Sasha's children. While there is little doubt that Tchaikovsky did feel strong homosexual attraction to boys, it was something that he knew how to keep within bounds and he never let it descend into paedophilia. Instead it was channelled into a deep love of those who came into his care, like Kolya, the deaf-mute boy who was Modest's tutorial charge and whom Tchaikovsky had nursed through the effects of drinking the polluted water in the south of France a few weeks before. Combined with the loneliness which had been growing worse for the last two years at least, these intense feelings convinced him that he must have a family of his own, the sexual aspect of life with a woman being far outweighed by the prospect of a stable and responsible life. At 36 he resolved to marry and settle down. It was an entirely understandable resolution. Its fatal flaw, though, aside from the true depth of his own sexual personality, was the fact that he was even more at sea than most men when it came to selecting women. If he had been capable of abjuring homosexual liaisons, which were becoming talked about behind his back and which Sasha suspected but forgave, he should have said yes to Vera Davidova and tried to make something of her dreams, most of which he shared. But he was not capable of disregarding his nature and for a man as complicated as Tchaikovsky, the Vera solution would have been too simple. It was no longer an option in any case, for she had been married for several years.

Nothing was attempted yet, however, and when he returned to Moscow the usual routine was set in motion once again. Thoughts of marriage still dominated his correspondence with Modest and Sasha, both of whom were against the idea for very different reasons; Sasha because she did not believe he was thinking the proposal through properly, Modest because, as a fellow homosexual, he knew the scheme would never work. In Tchaikovsky's own mind the paramount urge for fatherhood had been replaced, in the comfortable isolation of his own flat, with a desire for a purely legal arrangement with a woman who would be prepared to help him silence the rumours without risking his 'peace and freedom'. It was an unlikely recipe.

For the first time in many years he returned from the summer visits without a major new work in his luggage and the break from significant composition continued during the autumn. There was a popular success, though, with the *Marche Slave*, written in a bout of patriotic sympathy for the victims of the Serbian-Turkish war which had broken out in the Balkans. Tchaikovsky, using Serbian tunes as the basis of the march, caught the mood of fervent Slavonic fellow-feeling perfectly, though he was not deluded enough to think that there was any great musical worth in the piece.

By the time of the march's performance on 17 November Tchaikovsky was deep into another orchestral work in the series of *Romeo* and *The Tempest*. Initially he had looked for an opera subject but this had been scaled down and while he was enduring Vichy, Modest had written suggesting a scheme for a work based on the stories of either *Hamlet* or *Francesca da Rimini*, the woman from Canto V of Dante's *Inferno* who was murdered by her husband when caught in the arms of her brother-law. In October Tchaikovsky settled on *Francesca* as the appropriate character, inspired not so much by the story as by Gustave Doré's dramatically mannerist engravings from 1860, with their swirling serpentine figures carried along in the whirlwinds of

Gustave Doré's illustration of
Francesco da Rimini in Canto V
of Dante's *Inferno*, 1861.

the hell reserved for disastrous lovers. Given his own
tempestuous emotional state at the time, the subject is of greater
significance than the details of the programme around which
the Symphonic Fantasy is constructed. He completed the score
on the same day that the *Marche Slave* was first performed and
in its turbulence it is the only one of Tchaikovsky's works which
is influenced by Wagner's musical world, a debt which was
acknowledged but wondered at, given the miserable impression
made by the *Ring*. On the other hand, since Tchaikovsky made
some of the sketches for *Francesca da Rimini* on the journey home
from Bayreuth, it is hardly surprising that something of the
musical banquet he had heard stuck in the mind.

With the applause for the *Marche Slave* still ringing in his ears, Tchaikovsky headed for St Petersburg where *Vakula the Smith* was at last ready to be unveiled on 6 December 1876. As with so many competition-winning compositions the reaction to *Vakula* was precisely opposite to that of *The Oprichnik* – critical success and audience indifference. The contrast between the two productions could hardly have been more marked. Where *The Oprichnik* had been hurriedly and shoddily produced, *Vakula* had time and money lavished on it and was given a far better production than usual. Where Cui, Laroche and Tchaikovsky himself had hated *The Oprichnik* all agreed that *Vakula* was a fine work. Where *The Oprichnik* had run well in the capital and transferred even more sucessfully to the provinces, *Vakula* limped on in the repertoire for three seasons without inspiring any great affection.

Tchaikovsky seems to have greeted the failure with equanimity, settling down to write, before Christmas, one of his sunniest, most enduring and least troubled works, the *Variations on a Rococo Theme* for cello and orchestra. It is possible that the piece was commissioned or at least requested by the German Moscow Conservatoire professor who gave the first performance nearly a year later, Wilhelm Fitzhagen. If there is a reaction to *Vakula the Smith* it is that there is barely a trace of Russian influence in the work. It does though, start another trend to which Tchaikovsky returned several times in future years, the affectionate look back to the musical world of the eighteenth century. The theme of the *Variations* is a jolly piece of pastiche, whatever its origins, which allows him to exploit the skittish qualities of the cello as well as its cantabile possibilities. The work we hear today is not as Tchaikovsky intended it, however, for Fitzhagen altered it drastically before publication. Tchaikovsky had given him permission to make some minor technical alterations to the solo part but the player went far further, changing the order and cutting the final variation altogether so that the work was a more spectacular vehicle for his virtuosity. It was an attitude not unusual in nineteenth-century soloists and, although Tchaikovsky was upset by the mutilations, he did nothing to prevent the 'improved' version appearing in print and becoming the standard reading.

While he was writing the *Rococo Variations*, Tchaikovsky met Tolstoy for the first and only time, at a soirée organised in the writer's honour by Rubinstein. On the programme was Tchaikovsky's *First String Quartet*, with Fitzhagen playing the cello part. It moved the great man, who sat next to the composer, to tears; an effect which gave Tchaikovsky immeasurable pride. When Tolstoy returned home he sent the composer some songs in settings he had been given, hoping that Tchaikovsky would make something of them. His musical taste was not as sure as his literary taste, however, and politely but firmly Tchaikovsky wrote back that they were too far from the originals for successful treatment, though he promised to consider them as themes for use in a symphonic setting.

It was in this atmosphere of normality that 1876 ended and

Swan Lake in its 1877 production, which achieved nothing like the success that it did later.

in the first months of 1877 there was no inkling that it would be a year that signalled anything other than continuity. In the last two days of the year he had his first correspondence with Nadezhda von Meck, a wealthy widow who had commissioned some violin and piano arrangements for the domestic musicians she employed. News came from Vienna and Paris that *Romeo and Juliet* had found no favour: Vienna, then as now the most conservative and closed-minded city in Europe especially hating the work, which was hissed at the Vienna Philharmonic. Undeterred, and with a reborn sense of confidence, Tchaikovsky allowed himself to be persuaded to conduct the *Marche Slave* at the Bolshoi at the end of February. This time his head did not fall off, or even feel as if it was going to, and Tchaikovsky was sufficiently cheered by the experience to announce that in future he would positively seek opportunities to direct his works, though he did so only rarely for several years yet.

Swan Lake was premiered on 4 March 1877, the proceeds going to the first Odette, Pelagaya Karpakova, as a benefit. It was not a success. The scenery was substandard, the choreography by Julius Reisinger was uninspired and the conducting was uncomprehending. It was not an auspicious start for a work which has become an indispensable part of the tradition of dance, re-interpreted by choreographers throughout the twentieth century in ways which reveal it as having depths nobody, including its authors, suspected at its first production.

The same night that *Swan Lake* was unveiled the *Second String Quartet* reached St Petersburg and within the week *Francesca da Rimini* was premiered. Rubinstein conducted two performances in Moscow, though it was to be a year before Napravnik introduced it in St Petersburg. Moscow audiences were delighted, however, and the spring arrived full of promise for the composer without a sign that the turmoil of *Francesca* was about to be mirrored in his own life. It was the month, too, that the first thoughts for a new symphony, the fourth, began to take shape. It was to prove to be a work that not only signalled a new depth and sense of personal involvement in his writing but one which lifted his symphonies into an entirely different league.

Chapter 7

Great Opera, Great Disaster

Three events coincided in the spring of 1877 to bring Tchaikovsky's emotional life to a point of crisis. Two of them turned out to be entirely for the good but one brought him a degree of pain and with it self-knowledge from which he never recovered. In all three experiences Vladimir Shilovsky, by now aged 25, was the agent. In April he was married to a Countess, a strong personality of his own age and with just as much money. We do not really know whether Shilovsky had ever been Tchaikovsky's lover but there is much in the relationship – the irritation, the frequent visits, the age and intellectual gap, the jealousy and finally (after Shilovsky's marriage) a catty dispute over money – to suggest that there can have been few other reasons for the two to have been so close for so long. His marriage, although it had been long planned and was intended to be dynastic in uniting two impressive fortunes, was still a shock to Tchaikovsky when it actually happened and confirmed him in his own resolution that he must follow the same path if he was to find respectability and peace of mind.

In the same months Nadezhda Filaretovna von Meck had become more than a chance supporter and occasional commissioner of domestic trifles. It is difficult in a short space to do justice to the complicated and peculiar nature of their relationship, which was deeply intimate and which brought Tchaikovsky a measure of financial stability for more than a decade. It seems that from the beginning she realised that he needed money and that she was in a position to help. Tchaikovsky had been borrowing heavily, despite the fact that his Conservatoire salary was good and that his compositions earned him an increasing amount. Nonetheless he was used to moving in the upper echelons of Muscovite society and although he had no dependants and often enjoyed the hospitality of friends and family, he still lived beyond his means. He was also, in his turn, generous as a friend and lent or gave money that he could not really spare. Over the years he

Nadezhda von Meck, Tchaikovsky's reclusive and enigmatic patron.

had borrowed over 7,000 roubles from Shilovsky, a fact which made him uncomfortable on all fronts, and he had also borrowed from money-lenders when he felt he could not keep asking his wealthier friends.

Nadezhda von Meck provided a delicate way out. She was nine years older than Tchaikovsky. Before she was 17, she had married a railway engineer, Karl von Meck. He had, after her prompting and like Tchaikovsky's father, tired of working for the government and become one of the pioneers of the Russian

Tchaikovsky photographed with his wife, Antonina Milyukova, in the brief weeks they spent in unhappy marriage in 1877.

Railway system in the 1850s, making them immensely rich in the process. The engineering background was one shared piece of heritage. Of more importance, though, was the fact that Nadezhda had grown increasingly appalled by sex and marriage, despite – or perhaps because of – bearing eleven children. She despised social life, viewed her own interests as firmly 'masculine' in character and found great emotional satisfaction in having a friend with whom she could communicate thoroughly without initially having to suffer the inconvenience of having her passion disabused by physical acquaintance. This suited Tchaikovsky even more, for he wanted a substitute mother, not a female lover, and a sensitive patron who believed in his genius, whatever his personal state. They took their desire for isolation to extremes. Not only did Nadezhda never meet Tchaikovsky – though they came across each other

102

once by accident in the woods but passed on by without exchanging a word – she never met his relatives either, even though her son Nicholai married his niece, Anna Davidova. In the months ahead her supportive detachment, and her entirely cynical attitude to marriage, did more than anything else to keep Tchaikovsky's distress within manageable bounds.

The third occurrence was a classic coincidence of mistimed fate. As early as 1865 Tchaikovsky had met a 16-year-old girl called Antonina Milyukova at a gathering of mutual friends – her relations, his school connections. The impression he made was tremendous and it was increased when, several years later, she enrolled at the Moscow Conservatoire. She was of good family but poor and had to earn her own living, probably as a seamstress. By 1875 she had left the Conservatoire without having shown any usable talent. She was just one of the host of young ladies of gentility who were the backbone of the Conservatoire's student population but of whom little was expected or, in all probability, encouraged. They were the make-weights in a male-dominated profession which, nonetheless, needed their fees to survive. Tchaikovsky, it seemed, noticed her in class no more than he had done at their first meeting. She was just a girl in the crowd.

For Antonina, however, the story was very different. All through her teens and twenties she carried the image of Tchaikovsky with her; good-looking, urbane, funny and incredibly talented, writing music that, she had been told, stirred people like nobody else in Russia. He was also affectionate, as he was with so many of his students, and treated the female ones with the sort of kind warmth that perhaps only a homosexual teacher can do without raising fears or suggestions of impropriety. Antonina was not clever or talented but she was hard-working, honest and devoted, going every day for six weeks to chapel to pray for the musician with whom she had fallen so desperately in love. She put his failure to respond with anything more than his usual affability down to shyness. It was a reasonable mistake to make, for he was shy and his true sexual inclinations, though on occasion hinted at obscurely in the more unsavoury sections of the press, were by no means common knowledge. After her six weeks of prayer she plucked up her courage and wrote to him, pouring out the accumulated love. To her amazement and delight he replied immediately. To his delight, she seemed the answer to the problem that had been preoccupying him ever since he returned from the visit to Modest the previous summer: how to give himself the trappings of family without marrying someone

Klimentova Muromtseva, the first singer to play Tatiana's Letter Scene, from the 1879 production of *Evgeny Onegin*.

strong or sharp enough to interfere with his life of composition and occasional homosexual indulgence. Antonina knew enough about music to understand the basic process. She was from a decent family but not, he thought at first, encumbered with demanding relatives, so might fit in well at Kamenka and with the rest of the Tchaikovsky and Davidov clan. Above all she was 28 and he was just 37; both had good reasons for wanting to marry quickly.

We do not have his letter of reply but later in the sequence it is clear that he was having second thoughts and that, even having taken the decision to marry in principle, he was still not ready to face the emotional demands that a relationship with a woman – even a superficial one – was inevitably going to involve. Tchaikovsky seems to have replied pointing out some of his shortcomings, though clearly not the most important one, and then to have left Moscow for a few days with Konstantin Shilovsky, Vladimir's brother. He failed to tell Antonina or see her before he left, reducing the lovelorn girl to ever more desperate protestations of love, to the extent of declaring that she could not live without him and would soon kill herself. This does not seem like a serious suicide threat, as it is often interpreted (including, when explaining his actions later, by Tchaikovsky himself) but rather a romantic excess to explain what she was going through.

Tchaikovsky returned from the country on 6 May and two days later went to see Antonina to calm her down. On 23 May there was a party at the home of Elisaveta Lavrovskaya, one of the Bolshoi company, who suggested writing an opera on Pushkin's 1833 novel, *Evgeny Onegin*, with its story centred on two letters declaring love, first from Tatyana and later from Onegin, and the miserable results of their respective rejections. During the following week Tchaikovsky became increasingly excited by the idea, had bought and read the book and sketched a possible scenario. At the end of the week he went to see Antonina once again and she reiterated her love. He promised to return the following day and it was this meeting, on 31 May or possibly 1 June 1877, which contained all the half-truths, misunderstandings, desires and promises which nearly destroyed them both.

Antonina's side of the story was written down the year after Tchaikovsky died. His tale was told by his friend Nicholai Kashkin 40 years after the events. Antonina conflates and renders the scene conventional – which, given their mutual inexperience and the formality of social niceties in late Tsarist Russia, it may well have been. Kashkin places the meeting firmly in the context of somehow living out or responding to the plot of *Evgeny Onegin*, a convenient story in which life's decisions were taken in order to avoid the dramatic conclusion of a work of art. This is surely romantic subterfuge and the sequence of events does little to support it. The points where the two versions coincide show that he took a sober, business-like tone which Antonina matched until the moment he actually proposed, at which point she did the obvious thing and threw her arms around him.

Whether Tchaikovsky told her that his feeling that he could not, at his age, expect to respond to ardent love, in fact excluded his enjoyment of young men is doubtful. Even if he had alluded to it in convoluted terms it is likely that Antonina would have neither picked up the insinuations or, wrapped up in the fulfilment of all the dreams of her twenties, listened very hard. His offer to love her in a calm, brotherly way was bound to be misinterpreted. He meant that he intended to do his marital duty and no more, that he would live an almost independent life with as little physical contact as was necessary to provide him with the family he craved. She thought it was just another side of his shyness and she made another fatal error in making no attempt whatever to interest herself in his music. It turned out later that she had never been to an RMS concert or heard any of his pieces. To her he was just the gorgeous Conservatoire professor she had set her heart on. Mundane was the word most used about Antonina. For a composer or any writer, deep interest in and comprehension of the work – even if it is not infallible or perfectly critically informed – is the precondition for a successful relationship. Domestic service is not enough. Yet her selfishness was nothing compared to his. She was intent on providing a happy, if dull, home for the man she had picked and that was expected to be sufficient. Pyotr Ilyich, on the other hand, was condemning to a life of abstinence a passionate and sexually active young woman, who was by no means bad looking and who, still a virgin at 28, was looking forward to discovering her own sexuality.

Tchaikovsky realised immediately that he was asking for trouble but he did nothing to retract his offer. For the rest of the month he busied himself with the exams at the Conservatoire and the libretto for *Evgeny Onegin*. The preliminary material for the *Fourth Symphony* was completed by 8 June, a week after his meeting with Antonina. However much he was in turmoil it was not affecting his ability to work, and anybody who listens to the exuberance of the symphony's pizzicato *scherzo* and the rumbustious finale, with its distinctly Russian motif and cascading strings, would not equate it with a month of torment and crisis. There is no denying that whatever the catalyst, the spring and early summer of 1877 saw Tchaikovsky produce some of the finest music of his life, of a quality that outstripped anything being written in Russia at the time except by Mussorgsky.

Immediately he could be free from the Conservatoire, Tchaikovsky headed for Glebovo, the estate of Konstantin Shilovsky, where he was provided with the ideal conditions for composition – a guest house entirely for his own use and that of his servant Alexei Safronov. According to Antonina, Tchaikovsky had the grace to seek her permission for the separation. So perfect was the routine – up at eight, work, breakfast, walk, work, dinner, walk and evening chat – that he made astonishing progress on *Onegin*, with the first scenes roughed out within days of his arrival. He reported this to Modest with the plan that he intended to stay at Glebovo till August, go to Kamenka and then take a trip abroad: no

mention of marriage and an accompanying wife. Well over half
the opera was drafted before he actually left Glebovo on 14 July,
a month earlier than he had suggested to Modest. One might
have thought that the peace and quiet of Glebovo, the
smoothness of the work on the opera, and above all the
isolation from all the emotional complications that Antonina
and his Moscow coterie represented, would have brought
Tchaikovsky to his senses. But it did not. Fundamentally it
clearly did not enter his head that if he was going to raise a
family, keep his wife content and stop the public speculation
about his sexual habits he was going to have to make love to a
woman. It was, after all, a sacrifice millions of women went

through with men to whom they were not attracted in order to achieve the same result.

Later he blamed obsession with the character of Tatyana and her letter scene in *Onegin* for his response to Antonina and his determination to see through the marriage. This may have had an element of truth but the gestation of the Letter Scene, perhaps the most powerful piece of vocal writing in Tchaikovsky's work, was influenced the other way round too, by the exploitation of Antonina's letters to him as well as the peculiarly intense epistolary relationship he was building with Nadezhda von Meck. In the same months that he was offering to marry Antonina it is likely from his letters that he was also having an affair with Josef Kotek, another ex-student and the young violinist who had brought him together with Madame von Meck. It is by those two more than by Antonina that the free-flowing music of *Onegin* and the *Fourth Symphony* were inspired. Indeed Antonina does not seem to have really inspired him to anything except tears and a desire to sleep on his own.

Kotek, along with Anatoly, were the only witnesses from Tchaikovsky's side when the marriage took place on 18 July, officiated at by Razumovsky, the priest who was also Professor of Church Music at the Conservatoire. Tchaikovsky almost collapsed when he had to kiss his bride and his state of tearful agitation continued on their first night, spent on a train journey to St Petersburg, during which he was calmed only by a chance encounter with Prince Meshchersky, one of his homosexual friends from his schooldays. In St Petersburg his father, now over 80 and living outside the city at Pavlovsk, was thrilled by his favourite son's new-found respectability but they lodged in the luxury of the Hotel Europa which was far more expensive than Tchaikovsky could afford. The inevitable opposition of the rest of the family and Nadezhda von Meck was parried by writing to them only just before the marriage took place. Antonina was entirely content, 'agreeable to everything and will never want more,' Tchaikovsky admitted. That only made everything worse. As well as feeling repulsed by her body he was bored from the outset by her unimaginative mind and did not even have the satisfaction of being able to argue that her demands were unreasonable. Visits from Nicholai Rubinstein, Bessel and Laroche just made him hate Antonina and the situation he had brought upon himself even more.

After a week in St Petersburg they returned to Moscow and then spent three days in the country with Antonina's mother, which was even less of a success than the honeymoon had been. Unlike Tchaikovsky's deep and close relations with his own family he found the Milyukovs quarrelsome and disputatious, with Madame Milyukova ever happy to denigrate the memory of her late husband. Back in Moscow his gloom was deepened further by news of the sudden death of one of his close friends from school, Vladimir Adamov. With intense relief he left for Kamenka and the warm familiarity of Sasha's house for the rest of August, leaving Antonina in Moscow to sort out their lodging for his return. He still felt that he would be able to calm down with Sasha, Modest and Anatoly (who unusually, were able to be there at the same time) and that the terror would recede once the idea of being married began to settle, even if there was nothing other than pity left in his feelings for Antonina. In Kamenka he did indeed calm down and after a while returned to work on the scoring of the *Fourth Symphony* and *Evgeny Onegin*.

Tchaikovsky did not return to Moscow until late in September, by which time he could no longer ignore his duties at the Conservatoire or his wife, who was beginning to fret. Even Tchaikovsky had to admit that she had worked hard and had made the flat they had taken 'elegant, nice and not without luxury.' For her part Antonina was pleased to have him back, relished the domesticity, delighted in the fact that she had her husband to herself and strove to make a good impression on his friends, though with little success. They found her pretty enough but bland, which was probably a fair assessment. Even at this distance of more than a century it is impossible not to feel anything but enormous sympathy for this poor woman who

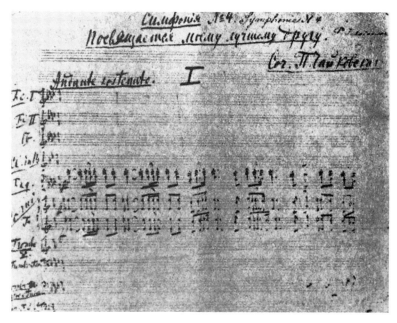

The opening of the *Fourth Symphony*, dedicated to Nadezhda von Meck.

109

A quartet of Tchaikovsky's students at the Moscow Conservatoire: from l. to r. Anatoly Brandukov, the cellist dedicatee of the *Pezzo Capriccioso*, Joseph Kotek, the inspirer of the Violin Concerto, Stanislav Bartsevich and Andre Arends.

had neither the mental nor physical equipment to enable her to deal with the neurotic genius for whom she had fallen in love and whose sexual tastes and experiences, when she found out about them, would have been utterly incomprehensible.

Antonina was prepared to be patient, however, confident that whatever the failures of their first attempts at sex, given time her husband would come to appreciate and love her as she wanted him too. Equally Tchaikovsky was vehement that the prospect was becoming more dreadful with every day. He wanted to die but not to commit suicide. After a week or two of domestic bliss in Antonina's care he attempted to make nature do the deed for him by walking into the cold waters of the River Moskva. Pneumonia conspicuously failed to develop, however, and he tried a more constructive ploy, telegraphing Anatoly to summon him to St Petersburg as if he was immediately required to supervise the revival of *Vakula*. His brother obliged, as ever, and on 6 October Tchaikovsky abandoned his wife and his students at the Conservatoire. When Anatoly met him at the railway station in St Petersburg the following morning he was in a state of near collapse. It was clear that heterosexual marriage was a torment with which he could not experiment any further.

It was decided that Nicholai Rubinstein and Anatoly should confront Antonina with the news that Pyotr Ilyich was not going to return. At first she seems to have been remarkably composed, being initially more impressed that Rubinstein, the head of her old college, was taking tea in her house, than with the import of the news. It is quite possible that, however blunt Rubinstein felt he was being, the message did not sink in immediately and she continued hoping that the rift would heal with time. Once it was clear that the separation was irrevocable she was never so amenable nor so lenient again. It was only from this point on that the hatred began on either side, though it seems a more mature Antonina was prepared to forgive him, though her subsequent life was far from easy. She never openly accepted the reason for his desertion, explaining it away as the result of pressure from his over-protective family, with whom she was – not surprisingly – highly uncomfortable. Given her inexperience and the ructions common in her own family, such a conclusion can be forgiven in a women who was less than perceptive. She believed that his emotional final good-bye at Moscow Station was the result of his being torn between her and his music and indeed this was the explanation to his sister that Tchaikovsky hid behind in the end. Antonina was right, though not in the way she expected. But if ever the world had needed evidence that Tchaikovsky was firmly homosexual it had it now. The only result of his attempts to gloss over the fact had been to make it plain to everyone who knew him. Someone in Moscow presumably made this plain to Antonina during the coming weeks, for she wrote a justifiably angry letter to Anatoly referring to it and in future years tried to extract money on the basis of it.

Anatoly, always the more sensible of the twins and, not being homosexual, less likely than Modest to inflame the situation, took his elder brother in hand and removed him to Switzerland, where they booked rooms in Clarens, near Geneva, in the early days of October 1877. There work began to flow again, the completion of *Onegin* and the *Fourth Symphony* proceeding together throughout November, December and January. Besides the music, he wrote long letters to Madame von Meck which were self-justifying attempts to excuse his marital conduct while at the same time inspiring her to grant him more

Modest Tchaikovsky (1850-1916) as a young man. Increasingly as the family's other artist and homosexual, he became Pyotr's closest confidante.

money. It is extraordinary how thoroughly he had come to depend on her financially and emotionally in only a year.

His letters to Modest in these months are revealing and not very pleasant. He becomes foul-mouthed towards Antonina as a combination of guilt and fear of exposure takes over. Neither was to diminish over the years. It affects his relationship with Sasha for the first time and whereas in the past he was always delighted to hear from her, now 'all letters from Kamenka are always disagreeable'. There was some reason for his misgivings in that Sasha, not understanding the depth of his abhorrence, had invited Antonina to Kamenka in an attempt to groom her into an acceptable wife for her brother. He begs Sasha to get rid of her and begs too for Modest and his young charge, Kolya Konradi, to join him in Switzerland once Anatoly has returned to Russia. Within a few weeks Sasha and Lev Davidov came to agree that Antonina's undeniably irritating qualities had finally defeated them too and the long-suffering Anatoly was called upon to escort her back to Moscow. Given her financial circumstances and the comforts of life at Kamenka she was none too keen to go, even though Tchaikovsky was giving her an allowance of 100 roubles each month. It is probable too that in Sasha she saw her last chance of bringing her husband back.

Meanwhile, as he pleaded poverty – even though Rubinstein had persuaded the Conservatoire authorities to allow him part-paid leave of absence – to Nadezhda von Meck, he and Anatoly went on an extended jaunt which took them to Paris, Florence, Rome and Vienna, about all of which Tchaikovsky constantly complained. Anatoly then returned to St Petersburg and his place as companion was taken by Tchaikovsky's servant Alexei, with whom he went back to Venice. The two of them spent January 1878 meandering through northern Italy – Genoa, San Remo, Milan (where Modest and Kolya Konradi joined them) and back to San Remo, where the *Fourth Symphony* was finished and despatched to Russia. *Onegin* was finished on 1 February. Much of the time he complained about lack of money. If so it was his own fault. He was still drawing a third of his normal annual money from the Conservatoire (all the while abusing Rubinstein to his brothers) and Nadezhda von Meck had not only paid off his debts but given him an allowance of 6,000 roubles, double his usual salary. In addition, he had refused a request from the Conservatoire and the Government to attend the Paris Exhibition as a paid official delegate. There had been added expense too, thanks to Alexei, who had contracted VD and had then to attend a clinic for a cure. February was spent ambling between Nice, Pisa and Florence before they settled back on the shores of Lake Geneva again in March.

The *Fourth Symphony*, dedicated deservedly to Nadezhda von Meck, was premiered by Rubinstein at an RMS concert on 22 February 1878, in Tchaikovsky's absence. It was not greeted ecstatically and Sergei Taneyev was forthright in his criticism when he wrote to his old teacher about it a month later, complaining about the influence of ballet music, the insubstantial qualities of the last movement variations and the sense that it was written to a programme. It was – as Tchaikovsky revealed to Madame von Meck – and the programme was a particularly self-pitying one about fate and living only through the happiness of others (which was what his patron wanted to hear). Tchaikovsky had the good sense not to encumber the work's first audiences with it. His reply to Taneyev was sensible and illuminating, comparing the basic pattern to that of Beethoven's *Fifth Symphony* and, citing Beethoven again as his precedent, reprimanding Taneyev for thinking that every piece of dance music with a cheerful tune had to be for the ballet and had no place in a symphony. It was a lesson that Taneyev could have learned to his advantage for it would have extended the shelf-life of his own rather stodgy and academic music.

The few weeks of inactivity during the winter of 1877-78 and the rather longer period since the summer when no new project had been embarked upon, came to an end in Florence. He was inspired by an erotic response to a young street-singer named Vittorio he had come across on a previous visit. There was no very exceptional result but the encounter did release his wish to compose again. He resolved to limber up by writing a piano piece each day, an intention which, if not carried out to the letter, did result in an impressive collection of thirty-six piano items and six songs between February and October 1878. These appeared as the *24 Easy Pieces* (à la Schumann) in the *Album for Children* Op. 39, the *Six Songs* Op.38 and the *12 Pieces* Op.40.

These were merely sidelines, however. Within four days in Clarens he had started work on two works of far greater significance: the *Piano Sonata in G*, Op. 37 and the *Violin Concerto*. Perhaps his most accessible work for the concert hall, the *Violin Concerto*, was another of those that he sketched in an astonishingly quick time, beginning it on 17 March and finishing on 11 April, effectively a week to each movement. It was one of those experiences which he tried to explain to Madame von Meck, admitting to her the futility of expressing,

'the boundless bliss of that feeling which envelops me when the main idea has appeared, and when it begins to take definite forms. You forget everything, you are almost insane, everything inside you trembles and writhes, you scarcely manage to set down sketches, one idea presses upon another.'

Pyotr Jurgenson (1836-1903), Tchaikovsky's main publisher in Russia and frequently his agent and financial rescuer.

That this was the case with the *Violin Concerto* there can be no doubt and once again Tchaikovsky was being a pioneer. Now that so many Russian composers – Glazunov and Prokofiev foremost amongst them – have contributed to the repertoire it is hard to remember that Tchaikovsky was the first. The preoccupation with Beethoven that permeates the *Fourth Symphony* may have been an influencing factor and the opening of their concertos have strong similarities: so too may the rather less academic inspiration of his affair with Josef Kotek. The young violinist was now studying with Joachim in Berlin and on 14 March he joined the Tchaikovsky party in Clarens. Work on the concerto began almost immediately. As so often in art it was the memory of the affair rather than its currency which was suggested by the concerto, for it seems that the sexual heat had gone out of their relationship by the time Kotek appeared in Clarens and Kotek in addition had developed a voracious taste for girls. Whatever their state of intimacy, though, he was a useful musician to have on hand for Tchaikovsky was not a violinist himself and Kotek's technical advice was invaluable, as Tchaikovsky himself was the first to acknowledge.

The first version of the work was finished within the month, exactly fourteen days after Kotek's arrival. There was a price to share for this facility, however, and all three – Kotek, Pyotr and Modest Tchaikovsky – agreed that the slow middle movement was not up to the standard of the outer pair. Another week saw another movement and this time Tchaikovsky produced one of the most poignant and affecting melodies of his career, music that provides a reflective coda to the emotional turmoil of 1877 and the winter that followed. There is, too, a passionate wistfulness to the first movement that suggests an awareness in Tchaikovsky that the work marks a new phase in his life. As he approached his 38th birthday, he had burned a lot of bridges the previous year.

By 11 April 1878 the *Violin Concerto* was scored – a work-rate which would leave any modern composer incredulous – and after a week of relaxation the party vacated Clarens. Modest had to take Kolya Konradi home, Kotek went back to Berlin and Tchaikovsky knew that, whatever the aftermath of his marriage, he needed Russia more than the untroubled luxury of life on the shores of Lake Geneva.

After a depressing train ride to St Petersburg, during which he was harassed by customs and Russian border guards, Tchaikovsky spent only a few days in the capital. It was long enough to find out, though, that his stay abroad and the public gossip about his private life had not done any damage to his professional standing, indeed, as so often happens, the whiff of a good story had made them that much more interesting. So Rubinstein had now swallowed fully his first reactions to the *Piano Concerto* and had performed it in St Petersburg to huge acclaim, even from Cui, and *Francesca da Rimini* had been played in March with similar approbation. Having been its most virulent critic, Rubinstein was now becoming the *Piano Concerto's* most doughty champion.

Tchaikovsky, Modest and Kolya did not linger in the city, however, but quickly made their way south to Kamenka, where they were joined by Anatoly who helped formulate proposals for a divorce from Antonina. Sasha gave her brother the welcome he had been longing for and during the weeks there, which included her name-day as well as his birthday, he did little more than toy with the *Piano Sonata* and pen a patriotic march for the beginning of the war against Turkey being waged on the Black Sea only 150 miles to the south.

Of more significance was his next move – to Brailov, the sumptuous von Meck estate a little to the east towards Moldova, near Zhemerinka. In line with their arrangement it was agreed that he should visit when Nadezhda herself was not in residence. He arrived there alone in May, having spent time with the family in Kiev, and found he was master of the house, its carriage, wonderful library, impressive (though, he candidly felt, unattractive) gardens and its extensive staff. His presence and relationship to the mistress of the house was not explained but his whims were to be accommodated and he was not to be disturbed unless he so wished. It was a strange way for Nadezhda to fulfil her, at this time, fervent love for Tchaikovsky but for her imagining his enjoyment of her pampering home was a potent fantasy.

In such surroundings, with an entire estate expressly devoted to making composition easy, Tchaikovsky set about producing music for his patron. The first two works were slight but tied up the loose ends of the winter. Two of the songs Vittorio, the Florentine street boy, had sung for him were complemented by four settings of texts Nadezhda had sent to Switzerland to form the *Six Songs* Op. 38. To the discarded first version of the *Violin Concerto's* slow movement, now recast as a Meditation, were added a Scherzo and a Melody to comprise the *Souvenir d'un Lieu Cher*, for violin and piano, a combination Tchaikovsky had once professed to hate and for which he had sworn never to write. The 'dear place' of the title was Brailov in theory, though Clarens lurked close, and the souvenir was to be Nadezhda's.

The third work composed at Brailov was more personal altogether. The subject of religion had surfaced several times in their correspondence and the events of the previous year had left Tchaikovsky more philosophical and more aware of his own mortality. In one extraordinary moment of self-revelation he balanced his own lack of faith in the dogma of the church with his equally fierce conviction that it was impossible, even after 23 years, that he would not have the chance to tell his dead mother that he loved her once again. His patron never fully became a replacement mother for him but she did offer some of the same characteristics: a distant and pure figure of love and a repository of confession. It was in this frame of mind, spurred by attending the services at the local convent, that Tchaikovsky embarked on his setting of the *Liturgy of St John Chrysostom*, the Orthodox equivalent of the Mass. Here again he was entering new territory, for the Imperial Chapel had a monopoly on church music and Jurgenson had to fight an extended and rancorous legal battle with the authorities before he was able to publish Tchaikovsky's contribution. It was a genre over which the fierce protectionism of the Imperial Chapel had presided for centuries. As a result, unlike the Catholic or Protestant traditions, there had been only very limited explorations of the possibilities of sacred music among Russian composers. For models they had been forced to look to the alien traditions of Italian renaissance polyphony and the classical world of Haydn and Mozart. These were largely inappropriate as Tchaikovsky realised, though tinges of both creep into his version of the liturgy. With his quiet enterprise he set out to repatriate the music of the Orthodox Church while producing a style unmistakably of his own time. He was only partially successful, and it was left up to Rachmaninov, in 1910, to produce the finest late romantic setting although Tchaikovsky's is a glorious attempt.

After the sojourn at Brailov he returned to Moscow for a few days, partly to face Rubinstein who, Tchaikovsky sensed, was becoming increasingly fed up with his overwrought Professor of Harmony, and partly to confer with lawyers about the practicalities of divorce. These turned out not to be very feasible, since they required a degree of co-operation and play-acting from Antonina which it soon became clear she was not prepared to give. In her mind she veered between hoping that Tchaikovsky could be persuaded to return to her and trying to extract as much money as possible.

With the legal and professional meetings over, Tchaikovsky returned to the Ukraine for the rest of the summer of 1878, commuting between Kondratyev's house at Nizy and the Davidov estates at Kamenka and Verbovka – where shooting, hunting and amateur theatricals occupied the extended family which had gathered. The only work which was possible was the tidying up of the various projects undertaken in the first half of the year – admittedly a prodigious collection – and their despatch to Jurgenson for an asking fee of 900 roubles for the entire lot. This batch included the *Piano Sonata* (which he finished on 7 August), the *Liturgy*, *Violin Concerto*, *Piano Album for Children*, *Twelve Pieces for Piano* Op.40, *Six Songs* Op. 38 and *Souvenir d'un Lieu Cher*. Of these he could ask 300 roubles for the Op. 40 pieces but only 50 roubles each for the *Sonata* and *Violin Concerto*, reflecting the relative values to a publisher of those with a domestic market and those which relied on professional performance.

When the crush and socialising at Sasha's became overwhelming in the middle of August, Tchaikovsky escaped to Brailov, Nadezhda being absent once again. There he explored the library and, after a few days enjoying the peace and quiet, buckled down to fresh composition once again. At first he was not certain what form the work was to take, other than that it was to be orchestral, but he produced the first drafts of three movements of something before the end of the month, starting with a scherzo. This was the last creative work of an extraordinary six-month period. If one adds to the list *Evgeny Onegin* and the *Fourth Symphony* the uncomfortable fact emerges that the most difficult 18 months of Tchaikovsky's life were also his most productive: a period of commitment, flight, exile and return in which he wrote at least two masterpieces (the *Violin Concerto* and *Onegin*) and a series of works which for any lesser composer would have been among the high points of a career.

Chapter 8

Independent Means

After a week in St Petersburg seeing Apukhtin, his niece Anna Davidov (who was enduring school there) and Anatoly, Tchaikovsky returned to Moscow in September 1878 as usual. However, none of the restlessness that had caused his marital crisis in the first place had been dissipated by the 15 months away. He began taking his classes as before although he knew that his heart was no longer in the job and that he was giving the students less attention than they deserved. The charms of Moscow which he had carefully constructed for himself over the years were now irretrievable. For the moment there was no sensible action to be taken, for Rubinstein was in Paris, ironically fulfilling the engagement to conduct at the International Exhibition that Tchaikovsky himself had turned down earlier in the year. Both the *First Piano Concerto* and *The Tempest* were on the programme, so Tchaikovsky could easily have ducked out of teaching and promoted himself in Paris, as Rubinstein had urged at the beginning. In fact Rubinstein had done his friend a big favour for the concerts at the Trocadero were a great success and, as Turgenev attested, Tchaikovsky was thrown into the limelight of international attention in a way that had never happened before.

   He determined to leave the Conservatoire staff before Christmas and attempt to live entirely on the proceeds of his composition and the continuing generosity of Nadezhda von Meck. It was a decision reinforced by an article he had read in the newspapers on the way back to Moscow. Part of it attacked Rubinstein's dictatorial way of running the Conservatoire and with this Tchaikovsky could not help but agree. He had been finding the way Nicholai Rubinstein treated him patronising for years – though not as objectionable as was the attitude of Anton. One other comment filled him with dread, however. The article talked in insinuating terms about the sexual relationship between the teachers and students and made clear that it was not just the girls that were affected. Tchaikovsky,

The programme for the
Russian concert at the Paris
Universal Exhibition, 1878,
when Nicholai Rubinstein
performed Tchaikovsky's
First Piano Concerto, about
which he had been so
dismissive at first hearing.

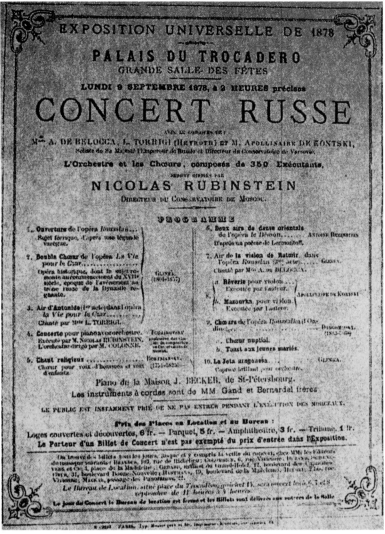

quite unnecessarily, took this personally. It was hardly
surprising given his current sensitivity on all matters of sex but
there seems never to have been any evidence that he formed
liasons with his students, at least until after he had a formal
teaching role. Nonetheless this and a thorough disillusionment
with the whole business of Conservatoire life was the basis for
his appeal to his patroness to free him from reliance on it.

Whatever Rubinstein's shortcomings he was a perceptive
director and a generous friend to Tchaikovsky. As soon as he
returned from Paris he made an impressive public speech in
which he waxed lyrical on Tchaikovsky's importance to the
Conservatoire and the wonders of the reception to his music in
France. Rubinstein then took his friend aside and quietly
discussed his plans for the future. Tchaikovsky was both pleased

120

and slightly miffed that Rubinstein raised no great objections to his departure and indeed understood that his protégé's time as a professor was now gone. His only insistence was that there be no sudden public resignation and suggested instead that Sergei Taneyev, for whom Tchaikovsky had immense regard, should be eased into the position in his stead over the course of the winter. It was a plan which confined Tchaikovsky to Moscow until Christmas but that was a bearable compromise since his musical business would keep him in the city at the start of the season in any case.

Rubinstein and the others were quick to realise that even this arrangement was not going to prove practical given Tchaikovsky's state of mind. In the event he took his last class on 18 October. On 20th a dinner was organised with those to whom he had been professionally closest in his Moscow years: Rubinstein, Nicholai Kashkin, Karl Albrecht (who had been perhaps the most steadfast and the least appreciated friend, for Tchaikovsky must have consumed many hundreds of roubles worth of food in his household over the years), Pyotr Jurgenson, his publisher and Sergei Taneyev, the most gifted and, in his time to come, the most influential of Tchaikovsky's pupils. With that he left Moscow, never to live there for any length again.

Even at such a moment of revolution Tchaikovsky was a creature of habit and his route over the following months took him to St Petersburg, Kamenka and Italy. In Florence Nadezhda von Meck had taken an apartment for him in the Villa Bonciani, only a matter of doors away from her own. As at Brailov every comfort was attended to, from a new grand piano down to flowers in the rooms on his arrival. She would look up at his window as she went for her morning drive, attend the same theatre performances (having bought the tickets), write to him every day, yet they never met. She understood that he would immediately feel trapped by such a meeting. He knew that he would soon find her constant presence in his immediate neighbourhood suffocating and that the spell would be broken if this peculiar doting obsession was allowed to descend into acquaintance. If the magic disappeared, he also knew, so would the subsidy. Instead he confined himself to favours like giving lessons to her demanding and not very talented newest 'find', Wladislav Pachulski, like Kotek an ex-Conservatoire student of his who was making himself indispensable to their patron in a servile way that Tchaikovsky could never have endured.

Composing soon reasserted itself as he accepted the situation – which was far from uncongenial, if a little odd. At first he tinkered with the orchestral suite he had started in the

Alexander Siloti, who studied with Liszt as well as Tchaikovsky and who became a noted interpreter of the latter's music, despite making unwarranted cuts in the Second Piano Concerto.

С. Петербургъ — St. Pétersbourg   Консерваторія — Le conservatoire

The grand premises of the
St.Petersburg Conservatoire.

summer but the movements that already existed had been left behind in Moscow by accident and progress on the subsequent sections was only fitful. He was more interested in the prospect of a new opera. Despite irritations that autumn with the St Petersburg and Moscow productions of *Vakula the Smith* and *The Oprichnik* respectively, he was drawn to another epic subject rather than the domestic world of *Onegin*. Perhaps he had been seeing too much Meyerbeer but whatever the spur, he settled on the story of Joan of Arc, a dangerous subject which was rarely handled well by composers.

In his case Tchaikovsky made things worse by constructing the libretto himself, basing it on a Russian translation of Schiller and a melange of French treatments. A third hand version of early romantic German drama does not promise to be satisfactory and Tchaikovsky was hardly the most obvious composer for the story in any case. *The Maid of Orleans* has the same feel of confectionery that clings to the historical subjects painted by the pre-Raphaelites at the same period. It would be unfair to say that he wasted his first season of freedom as a full-time composer, for *The Maid* has some fine music, but it does seem a strange lapse of judgement, after the extraordinary advance in *Onegin*, that he returned to such a stilted style of opera.

122

He had not yet heard *Evgeny Onegin* for, instead of entrusting it to the staff of the Imperial theatre – who would not understand it, he thought – Tchaikovsky badgered Rubinstein to have it tried out first by students at the Conservatoire. After much hesitation Rubinstein finally agreed and while Tchaikovsky was writing *The Maid of Orleans* in Florence and (once he had cut free from the von Meck bonds of luxury in the New Year) Clarens, *Evgeny Onegin* was prepared. The composer returned to Moscow to hear it, after a trip to Paris where he heard *The Tempest*, conducted well by Edouard Colonne, met with indifference at a morning concert in the Châtelet.

Even though Nadezhda von Meck continued to pay him, Tchaikovsky was constantly running out of money. He had to ask her for funds to go to Paris and again in Berlin – on the way back to Russia – he and Kotek found themselves short. This time he had the grace to try Jurgenson first but when that failed to materialise there was no option but to turn to his patron once again. Arriving back in Russia for the first time in six months at the beginning of March 1879, Tchaikovsky spent a few days on a round of family visits, one of them a sad duty to comfort Vera. After she had recovered from her passion for him she had married Ivan Butakov, a Vice-Admiral 16 years older than herself. Now she was distraught from the death of her five-year-old son and Tchaikovsky felt keenly for her. The tragedy rekindled their old friendship and over the following years he was a frequent guest, mixing with the aristocratic elite of Russian society among whom she now moved.

The first performance of *Evgeny Onegin* took place at the Maly Theatre on 29 March 1879. Although it was appreciated and although it was clear at the dinner given afterwards that his erstwhile colleagues at the Conservatoire were glad to have him back, there was no euphoria: nothing to suggest the importance that the opera was to play in Tchaikovsky's future reputation. He left the next morning for St Petersburg where the inevitable confrontation occurred with Antonina, which he had been dreading and trying to avoid for so many months. There was nothing accidental about it. She had clearly been planning to accost him and had watched Anatoly's house, waiting for the opportunity. On 5 April she called and asked to see him. Tchaikovsky spent two hours with her in the study, during which she begged him to live with her again, berating his relatives who kept him from her and trying to make him jealous by talking about the men who were in love with her but whom she was rejecting because of him. Eventually he gave her 100 roubles and told her to go back to Moscow and she agreed, though she had no intention of doing any such thing. Her lack of understanding of the true nature of their problem is obvious from her tactics. She had no comprehension of what his homosexuality (which by this time she knew about) actually meant in practice. To be charitable this is not as surprising as we might think. For one thing it is unlikely to have been a subject on which she had been educated, for another there were plenty of men in Russia – many of them friends of Tchaikovsky's – who led bisexual lives, indulging their preference for other men but maintaining marriages and family. It was what Tchaikovsky had intended to do when he had first married Antonina. It was in these circumstances that she resolved not to take no for an answer. She took rooms in the same building (in a ludicrous and unconscious parody of Nadezhda von Meck's habit in Florence and Paris) and wrote love letters to him. When he visited Moscow, she followed. Finally she and her sister cornered him and demanded a lump sum of 15,000 roubles to save her reputation and enable her to leave Russia. For plenty of good reasons – the fact that he did not have the money principal among them – Tchaikovsky refused.

The whole sequence affected his nerves and it was with intense relief that he left Moscow for summer and his usual round of visits in the Ukraine. There was no major new work in prospect but *The Maid of Orleans* had to be scored, as did the rest of the orchestral suite which he had put to one side before Christmas. The Ukrainian visit was not a complete respite from female demands, however. Apart from Sasha – who was perhaps the one woman he was consistently pleased to be near – Nadezhda von Meck was becoming proprietorial. She had offered him the use of Simaki, a cottage in the woods a couple of miles from Brailov, where he could compose without any of the distractions of the big estate or the danger of her passing by each morning. However the symbiotic proximity she craved led her to push for him to spend the whole summer there, relinquishing his habitual time at Nizy and Kamenka. Tchaikovsky was soon exasperated but he could not afford to antagonise his doting patron and a diplomatic way had to be found to deal with the problem. In this he failed and had to agree in the end to spend all of August in the vicinity.

The visit to Kondratyev at Nizy was sad too, for their old friend Nicholai Bochechkarov was there, clearly dying. Bochechkarov, although he has not surfaced in this book before, had been a constant element in Tchaikovsky's Moscow life. He had no money, depended entirely on the generosity of his many friends, was superstitiously eccentric and was already aged when Tchaikovsky had first met him ten years before. But he was also excellent company and when Tchaikovsky could stand the companionship of almost nobody else in his circle, he and Bochechkarov would dine together night after night. It was a friendship that demanded nothing of the other except good conversation, laughter and Tchaikovsky's willingness to pay for the food.

At Kamenka the young men he loved were getting themselves into trouble, though not with Tchaikovsky. Kotek arrived for a visit and set about flirting with all the girls in the Davidov household and news came from Clarens that the maid at the Villa Richelieu was pregnant by Alexei Sofronov. Tchaikovsky was delighted, regarding a child of his beloved Alyosha, as he nicknamed him, as his by extension. The father himself was rather less thrilled. There were other alarms and excursions. The alarms centred on Sasha who had been taken ill on a visit to Kiev and the excursions on Tchaikovsky's birthday, his 39th, celebrated with a picnic in the woods. There was a far sadder anniversary for the assembled Tchaikovsky children – Pyotr, Ippolit, Sasha and Modest. On 25 June they

Sasha and Lev Davidov with their children at Kamenka in 1880. At this stage the family was still reasonably stable, though Tanya (standing at the back) and Sasha were soon to show signs of distress.

commemorated a quarter of a century without their mother. In those years Sasha had borne the responsibility of a substitute as she bore all responsibilities, with fortitude.

Once at Brailov, Tchaikovsky took delight in the solitude of the woods that surrounded Simaki, where the river ran at the end of the garden, and worked steadily at the orchestration of *The Maid of Orleans*. The peculiar shield Tchaikovsky had built between him and his patron was revealed in all its strangeness during this visit to her estate. She would send him a daily schedule of her movements so that they would not stumble across each other. While he was busy plotting with her to introduce her sons to his nieces, he refused to meet her daughter when Pachulski (by now her factotum and his occasional student) offered to bring the girl over. When Nadezhda could assure him that she was not in the immediate vicinity he would go to the main house and play through his music on the piano, no doubt with her somewhere in earshot. One evening when there was a party and fireworks on the lake he was persuaded to sit across the water, in shadow but close enough to hear the conversation. Although at times they glimpsed each other – Tchaikovsky more than Nadezhda since she suffered from myopia – they contrived never to do so at the same moment.

This delicate arrangement only came to grief once that summer of 1879 – or at any other time in the 14 years they corresponded. One afternoon Nadezhda and her family were returning home through the woods in a line of carriages when, having misread the time, Tchaikovsky stepped out in front of them. There was a moment of confusion as they wondered how to proceed. Then the composer raised his hat, Nadezhda acknowledged him silently and the entourage continued on its way. In their letters they built the incident into a near calamity successfully averted and fierce measures were taken to stop any such thing happening again. It is clear from these letters that by this time the determination to avoid acquaintance was entirely on Tchaikovsky's side. Nadezhda was besotted with him and, for the financial imperative that she was his main source of income, he needed to keep it that way. He was no fool and he knew that if they met there would be no reason that he could explain why they should not become truly intimate. He was a bachelor, she was a widow. As far as she was concerned they had nothing to lose. For Tchaikovsky, though, the balance was critical. He knew that if ever she discovered that he could not live up to her expectations in person, then her generosity would cool with her ardour. She would find that the warmth that he sent her on paper (whether in letters or music) would never be matched by a physical counterpart and she would soon be just as confused and hurt as Antonina had been.

The wisdom of these precautions was revealed in the autumn when Tchaikovsky sent Nadezhda the four-hand arrangement of the *Fourth Symphony*, which was dedicated to her. She replied with a love letter which was as explicit as it was possible to be without alluding to physicality. She admitted being intensely jealous of him and pleased that his marriage had failed.

'I would have hated her a hundred times more if you had been happy with her. It seemed that she had taken from me what was mine alone, that to which I alone had a right because I love you as no one does, I value you more than anything in the world. ... Your symphony is the reason for me pouring out all this.'

Once the summer was over Tchaikovsky went to St Petersburg to advise Anatoly on his turbulent professional affairs, visit their father and help Sasha with her daughter Nataliya who was finding settling in at school as difficult as her uncle had done nearly 30 years before. From there he dropped down to Moscow, where he joined Nicholai Rubinstein and Pyotr Jurgenson, in theory to listen to the *Piano Sonata* and go through the accumulating proofs with his publisher, in practice to join them in some hard drinking. After which he headed back to a less frenetic life at Kamenka.

For once the decks were clear. He had no pressing work and for a week or two he enjoyed the freedom. But then boredom began to set in and he knew that he needed a substantial new project to rekindle his enthusiasm. The visit to Rubinstein and reports of his proven faith in Tchaikovsky's piano music was the trigger and by the middle of October 1879 he had started work on a *Second Piano Concerto*. Three weeks later, with the sketches of the immense first movement in rough form, he was travelling once again, first back to Moscow and St Petersburg and then on to Paris, where Kondratyev was staying and where Nadezhda von Meck had made all the preparations for his arrival.

He had installed himself sufficiently by the end of November to take up the Concerto once again, moving straight to the exuberant and rather Saint-Saëns-like final movement, the shortest of the three, before returning to tackle the slow middle movement, the Andante. By Christmas 1879 the concerto was basically complete. It is an amazing composition, and if less striking than the *First Concerto* at an initial hearing, the first two movements at least repay the trouble of a return. The opening movement, at over 20 minutes, is long enough to be a separate work and the first interpreters, Taneyev and Siloti, cut it significantly (Taneyev with Tchaikovsky's reluctant permission, Siloti without). The second movement – barely shorter than the first – the Andante, gives virtuoso concertante parts to violin and cello, making it into a triple concerto. It needs players of comparable calibre to the pianist and it is likely that Tchaikovsky expected Rubinstein to be joined by Fitzhagen and Kotek. Only the Finale, the shortest and least original movement, is conventional and, as is so often the way, it was the part of the concerto which appealed most to the work's first audiences. Its length, its unusual structure and the need to have either three soloists or section leaders in the orchestra of exceptional ability, has made the *Second Piano Concerto* unjustly neglected. Gerald Abraham's complaint in the 1940s that 'none of our concert pianists has apparently ever heard of it' is now wide of the mark – but not by much.

The *First Orchestral Suite* was given its premiere in Moscow to public acclaim on 20 December, by which time Tchaikovsky was arriving in Rome. Nadezhda von Meck had returned home, rather to Tchaikovsky's relief, and Modest was waiting for him in Italy. Once settled he set about seeing the sights and revising the *Second Symphony* for publication. Otherwise the new decade began badly. On 21 January 1880 Ilya Tchaikovsky died at the age of 85. His son was sad but not paralysed by grief. It had not been a completely unexpected event and Ilya had been frail for some time. Nonetheless he had lived an extraordinarily vivacious life: three marriages, one daughter well married, his three elder sons professionally successful and a career of his own which had lasted into his seventies and seen him rise to a position of respect and authority in the engineering world at a time when Russia was beginning to makes its industrial mark. Pyotr missed him but it was a gentle loss.

There was disappointment three days later when he found out from Colonne that the *Fourth Symphony* was to be played in Paris for the first time the next evening, giving him no time to get back to hear it. He never had heard the work and although he admitted it was his own fault for telling the conductor earlier that he would not be able to attend, he had hoped to be able to sneak in unrecognised. In the event the work was misunderstood by the Parisians, as he had feared. In those days it was the custom to applaud each movement, rather than judge the whole work, something which goes against modern ideas of symphonic unity. Then, however, conductors would judge the success of each movement in turn and repeat the more successful morsels later in the season. It was made clear by Colonne that he did not expect to direct the entire work again.

By the time that news reached Tchaikovsky, however, he was composing again, in a manner which showed that for once no news, bad or not, could distract him from the relative warmth of the Italian winter. He went back for inspiration to Glinka's excursions abroad and the *Spanish Overtures* written 35 years earlier. Tchaikovsky had spent a great deal of time in Italy but the *Capriccio Italien* is the first of his instrumental works to reflect the country directly. The *Capriccio* is a confection of the tunes encountered on his travels, including the fanfare which he heard from the nearby barracks every morning in Rome with which it opens. Tchaikovsky himself was aware that there is nothing very profound in the *Capriccio*, which explains its throw-away title, and that the merit was to be found in the orchestration, which was finished by May. This was the only piece of any substance to emerge from his winter in Rome. For the rest he scribbled five minutes' worth of 'crashes and bangs' for a Tsarist celebration which, to his relief, never took place and occupied himself for a lot longer than he would have liked with proofreading the badly copied vocal score of *The Maid of Orleans*.

In March 1880 he headed back to Russia, via Paris and Berlin. When he arrived at Anatoly's he found that he was much in demand. There were several performances of his music in prospect, the most notable being an entire concert in aid of the scholarship fund of his alma mater, the St Petersburg Conservatoire. Belatedly it was waking up to the fact that Tchaikovsky was its most illustrious graduate. The programme, on the 6 April 1880, was a potpourri of chamber, operatic and orchestral numbers, including the *First Orchestral Suite*, *Romeo and Juliet* and Tatyana's *Letter Scene* from *Onegin*. Of equal importance to his social standing was the insistence of the Tsar's brother and nephew, the Grand Dukes Konstantin, that they wanted to meet him privately. Tchaikovsky was overcome with nerves at first and only agreed to see the younger Grand Duke at Vera Butakova's home. In the event this was the start of an instant and lifelong friendship (though the offer of travelling around the world for three years was graciously declined by the composer) and the interview with the older Duke took place over a thoroughly congenial dinner. Once accepted by these royal eminences Tchaikovsky found that the rest of St Petersburg's aristocratic elite wanted a slice of him as well. He discovered to his surprise (and relief after the mess of his marriage, which he had thought would have stained his reputation) that he was becoming a social ornament among the various Princes and their daughters who dabbled in music. After a month of this he took the train down to Moscow for ten days of equally hectic activity with Rubinstein and his friends, interspersed with appointments at Jurgenson's to oversee publication details (which was the real reason for the visit). Before the beginning of May, though, he was on his way back to the Ukraine, from where he did not emerge until Christmas.

Paradoxically his new financial and geographical freedom – no job, no dependants, no property to worry about – were relaxing him well enough and turning him (as he hit his fortieth birthday) into something of a recluse but it was not the catalyst to great music that his patron must have expected. Tchaikovsky, it seemed, could compose very nicely when he was happy but he needed tension to produce music of indisputable worth.

There was a deliberate reason for the moderate production between 1880 and 1884. Tchaikovsky told Jurgenson in June 1880 that he had been writing too much; with too little self control, he might have added. He wished to write nothing but trifles for a year and instead revise and correct some of his earlier works while settling on new directions. Re-inventing one's creative personality is rarely an easy matter and though the intention showed a degree of intelligent self-criticism which goes beyond the usual hysterical view of Tchaikovsky, the attempt did not achieve a great deal. For the spring of 1880 he was left in sole charge of the assembled Tchaikovsky children at Kamenka and found dealing with adolescent girls as difficult as he found playing with their younger brothers and sisters delightful. He was not one of nature's schoolmasters and anarchy was soon the order of the day.

The feeling that quality had been sacrificed for quantity in his music persisted when he arrived at Brailov, the von Meck estate, for the latter part of the summer. Nonetheless as well as routine proofreading and revising work (including bringing *Romeo and Juliet* to its familiar form) he did turn his hands to a set of six vocal duets and another batch of songs, the *Seven Songs, Op. 47*. These were trifles, as he intended, but good ones and the motive may well have been to produce something that Jurgenson could sell, since as usual money was hopelessly short. The theory of independence, self-reliance and relaxation courtesy of the von Meck allowance was working out no better than any previous resolutions on financial stability.

Two compositions were produced in the autumn of 1880, though, which even if Tchaikovsky regarded them as trifles, the

Napoleon's army retreats from Moscow in 1812.

general public has since adopted as among his most famous, and in one case infamous, works. Considering his financial position and his feeling that he wanted to write nothing of any great depth, one might have thought a decent commission to come up with a piece for the 1881 Moscow Exhibition of Industry and the Arts would have been just the sort of task that Tchaikovsky would have found agreeable. In fact he regarded it with a distaste which has only been matched by that of the critics since. When the idea (which came from Rubinstein who had been put in charge of the music) was mooted by Jurgenson the answer was frosty. The choices for glorification were the exhibition opening, the consecration of a new cathedral (being built as a permanent memorial to the defeat of Napoleon in 1812) or the celebration of the Tsar's jubilee.

'...And it is impossible without repugnance to set about music which is destined for the glorification of what, at bottom, delights me not at all. Neither in the jubilee of the high-ranking person (who has always been fairly antipathetic towards me) nor in the cathedral, which I don't like at all, is there anything of the sort which could kindle my inspiration.'

In all his other letters on the subject of the overture, *The Year 1812*, he was just as dismissive, deriding it for its noise and banality even before he wrote the work. In the event he need not have worried about the appropriateness of celebrating the

131

reign of Alexander II. By the time the intended date of the performance came the Tsar had been assassinated. Still Tchaikovsky scribbled the music down in a week in October 1880 at Kamenka and spent a further month on the orchestration, which is its saving grace. However, although his own judgement was harsh, the *1812 Overture* is not a musical disaster. Tchaikovsky interweaves his ragbag of themes – the *Marseillaise*, the Tsarist anthem, folksongs, a snatch of *The Voyevoda* and orthodox chant – with the skill of a true craftsman. Not all of the work is bombast and gunfire. At least half is firmly in the tone poem tradition of Balakirev and Rimsky-Korsakov and close to his own programmatic music in *The Tempest* and *Francesca da Rimini*. If played in isolation few people would equate the intensely Russian and lyrical central section as being from a piece famous for bringing military hardware into the concert hall. And the descending cascade of strings which announces the final flourishes of bells, brass and percussion is as distinctive and effective at building tension as anything that he wrote.

The second work that he composed that autumn took longer to gestate and came from an altogether deeper part of his creative personality. This was the *Serenade for Strings*, Op. 48, and it is everything that the *1812 Overture* is not: tightly constructed, thematically inspired, emotionally contained and disciplined. The *Serenade* is also highly original. Only Dvořák's *Serenade* of 1875 is earlier in the line of late Romantic string writing, picking up from where the young Mendelssohn and Rossini had left off 60 years earlier. It is second, therefore, in the line that has gone on to include the great string pieces of Grieg, Suk, Elgar, Holst, Britten and Dag Wiren. Tchaikovsky's *Serenade* maintains the balance between lightness of touch, instrumental brilliance and gentle melodic elegance which so often eluded him but, when he achieved it, lifts him into the first rank. It is hardly surprising that it was the work that reconciled Anton Rubinstein to his most famous pupil's music.

Kamenka was no longer a refuge from real life and Tchaikovsky now had the cares of his sister's family to deal with. Sasha, more capable but just as highly-strung as her brother, had become a morphine addict (not uncommon or difficult to do in an age when it was given on demand in much the same way that tranquillisers were a hundred years later). The family finances were diminished by falling estate receipts and the emotional lives of the new generation in the Tchaikovsky maternal line were proving to be no less complicated than their parents. Worst of all his beloved servant

Alyosha was called up for army service, a trial that seemed to affect the delicate Tchaikovsky – who took comfort in drink, as he increasingly did – far more than it did the down-to-earth Safronov. At the end of November Tchaikovsky returned to Moscow for the first time since the spring and was delighted to be greeted within days by an enthusiastic performance at the Conservatoire of the *Serenade*.

In terms of public contact it was to be a busy winter for him. In St Petersburg *The Maid of Orleans* was at last due to be produced but Tchaikovsky was distracted by the emotion generated by visiting Aloysha in barracks. The conditions were grim but the lovelorn composer reacted with distress that verged on the hysterical. He had clearly forgotten the spartan

The title page for the original vocal score of *The Maid of Orleans*, Tchaikovsky's reworking of the Joan of Arc story.

conditions at school and in his brother's naval unit. Over the following months Tchaikovsky went to extraordinary lengths to use what influence he had to alleviate his servant's service conditions, befriending the commander of the regiment and working on his wife by accompanying her domestic singing. In Moscow *The Oprichnik* was resurrected after a period of political banning (it was felt to be inflammatory despite its frequent performance earlier; the Tsar was turning back to the bad old days of imperial control) and the *Capriccio Italien* was premiered on 18 December. Perhaps the performance that gave him most pleasure, though, was the concert performance at the Conservatoire of the *Liturgy of St John Chrysostom*. It was sung to a full hall and propriety was observed by a decree that there would be no applause at the end, just a presentation to the composer. It was a satisfactory way of snubbing the church authorities who were still dominated by the guardians of the Imperial Chapel monopoly.

Of more significance in the long term, though, was the first professional performance of *Evgeny Onegin* at the Bolshoi on 23 January 1881. It was given a decent production and, though the reviews were mixed and the public mystified by its unheroic atmosphere, it was recognised as a work of importance, even if not immediately accessible. It is an indication of the different theatrical taste of the nineteenth century that historical drama, often wildly improbable, was considered far easier for an audience to understand than a personal story from their own era. Tchaikovsky was not alone in making opera deal with a world which was roughly contemporary but it was still not accepted as the normal stuff of theatre.

In February 1881 there were two Tchaikovsky theatrical occasions in St Petersburg, neither an unqualified success. *The Maid of Orleans*, conducted by Napravnik, finally reached the stage of the Mariinsky on 25 February and was greeted by an extravagant number of curtain-calls, 24, for the composer and therefore also, almost inevitably, with one of Cui's more devastating tirades. Tchaikovsky did not hang around to read it, however, leaving the morning after the premiere for Florence and Rome. Four days before he had had to comfort Modest, whose first play to reach the official stage, *The Benefactor*, was closed after only one night at the Alexandrinsky Theatre. Clearly the family reputation was not yet invincible.

Chapter 9

Quiet Years

When he arrived in Rome in 1881, Tchaikovsky joined what would now be described as a "gay scene" but was then thought of as a gathering of independent Russian aristocrats and gentlemen escaping the winter. Kondratyev and Prince Golitsyn were already there by the time Tchaikovsky arrived and began to reacquaint himself with the pretty waiters and street boys he had spotted on his previous visit. With his usual servant partner away on military service the 40-year-old composer was alone to indulge himself as he wished. The trio of old friends were soon augmented by the younger generation of the Imperial family, led by the Grand Duke Konstantin Konstantinovich, who was commanding a battleship anchored

The Assassination of Tsar Alexander II in 1881 ended Russia's liberal reform.

at Ostia and who suggested that Tchaikovsky join them for a jaunt across the Mediterranean to Jerusalem, taking in Athens on the way.

This cosy set-up was shattered within two weeks, by which time Kondratyev and Tchaikovsky had dropped down to Naples, when news came from St Petersburg that Alexander II had been killed by a bomb on the very day that he signed a proclamation setting up the beginnings of representative democracy. His sons and nephew raced back from Italy to show solidarity with the new Tsar, Alexander III, who was as thick-headed and autocratic as his father had been intelligent and liberal. The signs were that he had all the rigid totalitarian instincts of his unlamented grandfather. The attempts at reform were soon eliminated and the chance of peacefully modernising the Russian constitution was lost for good. In the meantime, though, most Russians in the upper echelons like Tchaikovsky lost what liberal inclinations they had in their shock at the assassination and their fury at the revolutionaries and welcomed the crackdown on political freedom that followed.

Less far-reaching, but just as tragic, was the event that occurred ten days later. When news of the Tsar's death meant that the plan to tour with the Princes had to be scrapped, Tchaikovsky arranged to travel to Nice, where he was to meet up with Nicholai Rubinstein who, ill for some time with tuberculosis, had been ordered to recuperate in the sun. Instead he just reached Paris before collapsing and dying suddenly in his hotel. Rubinstein was only 46, yet his achievement had been not only the foundation of the Moscow Conservatoire and its impressive roster of teachers but the establishment of Moscow itself as a significant centre of musical life in Europe. More than most, Tchaikovsky had reason to be grateful to Rubinstein. Without his hospitality and championship it is unlikely that Tchaikovsky would have had either the finances or the encouragement to survive his early years in the world of music.

In Paris Tchaikovsky attended his friend and mentor's funeral at the Russian church, where he was appalled in equal measure by Anton Rubinstein's lack of grief and at the sight of Nicholai's distorted features in the open coffin. There was further bad news to come. For music the death of Mussorgsky from the ravages of alcohol five days after Rubinstein's demise was not a surprise but was seen by his contemporaries as a terrible waste of a great and original talent. Of greater concern to Tchaikovsky was the revelation that for the first time since her husband died Nadezhda von Meck was in financial

The death of Nicholai Rubinstein in 1881 threw the Moscow Conservatoire into years of turmoil and left Tchaikovsky without one of his most sympathetic supporters.

difficulty, though she hastened to reassure him that his allowance was not in danger. It was in sombre mood indeed that he returned to Moscow, where there was pressure for him to take over from Rubinstein as Director of the Conservatoire. Wisely he refused and made his way back to Kamenka. There his sister's continuing illness and his brother-in-law's business commitments meant that he had to make himself into a substitute parent once again and composition remained impossible until May 1881.

Two projects emerged after May – one immediate, one for later: an operatic version of Pushkin's poem *Poltava*, for which a libretto had been commissioned for a fellow composer by the Imperial theatres but then abandoned. For the time being, though, he needed a different sort of project, as far from the artifice of the theatre as possible. The trials of the previous few months had shaken Tchaikovsky and sent him back to his spiritual roots for comfort. It seemed as though a composer who had been brought up and flourished in the climate of western liberalism of Alexander II's reign reacted like the rest of Russia to his assassination, with a need to re-establish his links with the roots of his country. If this was not autocracy or folksong, it had to be the Orthodox Church and Tchaikovsky set himself the task of researching, then setting a service of Vigil, the equivalent to the Vespers of the Catholic Church. It was no easy task because there seemed to be few precedents and little agreement among the clergy as to the proper order of service.

This tranquil task was interrupted by the problems of Sasha, who was now mixing morphine, alcohol and chloroform, and her daughter Tanya, who was distraught after breaking off her engagement to a man in Moscow because his improper advances had come close to rape. Alyosha was given a further draft period in the army by the new Tsar Alexander's edict that the current three year service period was too soft. It was promptly doubled. In August, Tchaikovsky and Alyosha (on leave) intended to escape to Simaki, the cottage on Nadezhda's Brailov estate, for a month of solitude. It was not to be, though, for it soon became clear that despite Lev Davidov's attempts to intervene on the von Meck family's behalf, Brailov had been so badly managed that it would have to be sold. At the same time Alyosha's leave was cut and he was forbidden to leave the Moscow region. A year which should have been peaceful and carefree was turning into a nightmare for Tchaikovsky and all those to whom he was closest. The only good tidings came from the unlikely source of Antonina who had found a lover capable of giving her some satisfaction at last and had become

Tanya Davidova, Sasha's eldest daughter, who was causing the family, especially her uncle Pyotr, real concern by the time she was 20.

pregnant, so relieving the pressure on Tchaikovsky to have to fake grounds for divorce.

To be with Alyosha, Tchaikovsky returned to Moscow for a month where the pressure for him to return to the Conservatoire, still rudderless after Rubinstein's death despite the appointment of Nicholai Hubert as Director, became intense. Again Tchaikovsky successfully resisted, pressing Sergei Taneyev's claims to the Professorship instead. For once he was entirely right. Any inspiration he might have given his students was offset by his own distaste for the work and even as a figurehead he would have not been much use unless prepared to spend some time there, which he was not. Musically the only activity after the music for the Vigil was not his own. At

Jurgenson's request – and for a decent fee – he arranged and edited the complete sacred works of the greatest figure in eighteenth-century Russian church music, Dmitri Bortnyanski (1751-1825).

Back in Kamenka the Davidov family was in crisis. Sasha was despatched to Yalta for a cure but her place as the family addict and hysteric was soon being taken by Tanya, only 20 but increasingly unstable. Soon it was clear that mother and daughter were stoking each other's self-destructive tendencies. They both needed help but these were the days of mineral baths and rest-cures, not clinical psychiatry. Tanya's sister Vera escaped the estate in spite of this and married a young naval officer who by remarkable and disconcerting coincidence was also called Nicholai Rimsky-Korsakov. Predictably the trials and tribulations of Sasha and her five girls were beyond Tchaikovsky's sympathies and it was the two younger boys, Dmitri and Vladimir (always known as Bob), aged eleven and ten respectively, with whom he felt at home.

The winter routine was becoming settled too. In November 1881 he went back to Florence, where the game of proximity but no contact with Nadezhda was played out again for a few days, and then joined Modest and Kondratyev in Rome. This meant that he missed the long-awaited premiere of the *Violin Concerto*, given not by its inspirer, Kotek, or by its next dedicatee, Leopold Auer, but by Adolph Brodsky, the young genius who came to dominate Russian violin playing for the next 30 years. He introduced the concerto at his début with the Vienna Philharmonic (conducted by Hans Richter) on 4 December 1881 and it attracted one of the most vicious and unwarranted critical attacks in the history of music. Written by Eduard Hanslick, who hated all traces of nationalistic writing, especially Russian, it dubbed the concerto stinking music. Tchaikovsky never forgot the review but happily the rest of the world did, largely thanks to Brodsky's continuing championship.

The change of scene and the completion of his work on Bortnyanski made serious composition seem a possibility once again. Despite the relative failure of *The Maid of Orleans* and the less than rapturous reception his work for the theatre received in comparison with his orchestral and chamber pieces, Tchaikovsky was determined that he should return to opera. The question of a subject and libretto was more intractable. He had been toying for some time with Pushkin's *Poltava*, to which he had been granted the libretto rights, but he was doubtful about whether it would fire him sufficiently. He was drawn as well to the idea of returning to *Romeo and Juliet*, since he could look to his own fantasy overture for the basic thematic material. A story by Averkiev, *Vanka the Steward*, caught his attention when he saw a dramatised version at the theatre in Kiev. This would have taken him into the same territory as *The Voyevoda* and *The Oprichnik* but it was the first of the ideas to be discarded. In an indecisive way he dabbled with potential arias and love scenes through the winter months of 1881 without achieving anything significant.

More fruitfully, he turned to an idea which Nadezhda von Meck had been urging on him. She had hired a young pianist for a few months the previous winter, Claude Debussy (a pattern of seasonal employment that continued for a further two years), to join her other musical servants in a trio. Debussy had been made to work his way through all the Tchaikovsky pieces in the household by his patron and to make arrangements of some of them. However there was nothing in the output for piano trio, the favoured medium of the establishment. It was a form that Tchaikovsky had already said he loathed. Now though there was another consideration than the entreaties of Nadezhda. He wanted to commemorate Nicholai Rubinstein by writing an intimate work which his interpreter would have enjoyed performing. It also offered the opportunity of getting the creative processes working again while the opera project was sorted out. The *Piano Trio* was started in Rome and was finished within a few weeks, by the middle of February 1882.

With the chamber music despatched to the publisher and dedicated to 'the memory of a great artist', Tchaikovsky finally dropped the idea of setting *Romeo and Juliet* (perhaps because Gounod had already done it) and opted for the Pushkin, retitling it *Mazeppa* after its hero. Apart from the drama of Pushkin's poem, Tchaikovsky had enough personal connections with the subject matter to make it attractive. Ivan Mazeppa (1644-1709) was the western-educated leader of the Ukraine who, having delivered his country into Russian hands, fought against the Tatars with Prince Golitsyn (an ancestor of Tchaikovsky's old friend) and sided with Peter the Great, then changed his mind and allied instead with Sweden during Peter's war with Charles XII. It was effectively the defeat of the Swedish-Ukrainian forces at the Battle of Poltava in June 1709 that cemented Peter's dominant position in the region and ended Swedish expansion. Poltava lies about a hundred miles east of Kamenka, in a region Tchaikovsky had come to know well.

This affinity, however, was not enough to fire him as *Evgeny Onegin* had and he struggled with *Mazeppa's* composition all through 1882, interrupted constantly by the needs of his relations. Anatoly, just 32, was married in April – to the daughter of a well-off Moscow family – and Tchaikovsky found himself in his congratulations to his brother lamenting his own inability to love a woman and the parallel longing he felt to be comforted by one. It does not take too much psychology to see that it was his mother he was still missing. At Kamenka the disintegrating Davidov family were barely in residence, leaving the estate for the most part to Pyotr, Modest and Kolya Konradi. The sudden death of the latter's father meant that the 14-year-old deaf-mute was now the master of a large estate at Grankino. Modest, who had virtually brought the boy up on his own and had ensured that his affliction had not hampered his education, was left 10,000 roubles. Tutor and pupil departed to tend to their affairs and Tchaikovsky joined them a few weeks later when the arrival of the Davidovs in force meant that there was no longer space or quiet to work.

Except for a visit to Moscow in August 1882 – about which Tchaikovsky complained as usual – he spent most of the time until November at Grankino and Kamenka. The trip to Moscow was worth making, however, for his works were at the centre of the music programme of the Moscow Exhibition. Brodsky introduced the *Violin Concerto* to Russia, Taneyev performed the *Second Piano Concerto* and the *1812 Overture* was given its first outing. Once back in the Ukraine *Mazeppa* continued to give him trouble through the autumn and, when the sketches had been finished, he found he was delayed from work on the orchestration by a demand from St Petersburg to recast the role of Joan in *The Maid of Orleans* for mezzo-soprano, a task which required far more rescoring than the theatre directorate realised. He found himself becoming more and more irritated with life at Kamenka: the industrial stench which drifted from the factories by the river and the behaviour of his niece Tanya, now in the grip of eating disorders and morphine addiction, who spent much time dallying with the resident music-teacher by whom she promptly became pregnant (though Sasha and Lev were never told and the entire affair was handled by Modest, Pyotr and Nicholai Tchaikovsky). For Tchaikovsky, who was appalled by women's sexuality, this was the last straw. Tanya's condition was easy to understand – a cry for attention from the eldest of eight children – but hard to cure and impossible to live with.

In November he escaped to Moscow and from there to Berlin and Paris, where at last he felt he could relax safely and finish *Mazeppa*. The relief was short-lived, however, for when Modest

Adolph Brodsky (1851-1929), the violinist who first performed the *Violin Concerto* in public.

141

arrived he brought Tanya with him, hoping to find a neurological cure for her psychological problems. There was interruption of a different sort with commissions, which there was no refusing, for three pieces for Alexander III's coronation. Despite the new Tsar's unpleasantly military view of the world he was very partial to Tchaikovsky's music – ever since the *Festival Overture* written for his marriage to Princess Dagmar of Denmark – and had sent the composer a gift of 300 roubles on his accession (somewhat more welcome than the cufflinks had been twenty years before). Tchaikovsky reluctantly obliged with an arrangement from Glinka's *A Life for the Tsar* of a chorus for 7,500 voices, a march and a cantata, *Moskva*, for two soloists, chorus and orchestra.

Tchaikovsky remained in Paris working on *Mazeppa* until it was finished two days after Tanya's son was born on 8 May 1883 (and the day after his own birthday) and then returned to Russia. For once he did not spend the summer in the Ukraine but with Anatoly's new family outside Moscow. Anatoly's wife, Praskovya, was only 19 and outlived the entire generation of her family, dying in 1956 at the age of 92. It was a huge relief to be somewhere away from the convulsions of Sasha's household and best of all Alyosha, recovering from a serious bout of pneumonia, had returned to the fold. Tchaikovsky was also near enough Moscow to visit (and be visited by) old friends without losing his country routine of working and walking. Meanwhile he mediated in the turmoil of the Conservatoire, for Nicholai Hubert had lasted less than two years as Director. The one encouraging piece of news from Kamenka was that Sasha's daughter Anna was to marry Nadezhda von Meck's son Nicholai, a piece of matchmaking in which Tchaikovsky and his patron had been indulging for years, though with different potential Davidov brides.

The stay in Paris and Tanya's expenses had drained his finances and Tchaikovsky bluntly replied to the offer of a gift worth 1,500 roubles from the Tsar (in recognition of the coronation music) that he would rather have the money. The Imperial household did not operate like that, however, and a fine diamond ring was duly sent. Tchaikovsky repeated the exercise with the cufflinks and pawned the bauble for 375 roubles, went out for a drink and promptly lost his wallet, together with the pawn ticket. He was not in a position to find the poetic justice in the event funny and turned in desperation to Nadezhda for 1,000 roubles. She responded but she too had her troubles, for her youngest son had died of heart disease at the age of twelve only weeks before. Tchaikovsky's response was unusually restrained. There were times when his selfish side could be thoroughly unattractive.

Proofs of *Mazeppa* soon began to arrive and needed extensive revision but Tchaikovsky felt that this was not enough creative stimulation and set about sketching a *Second Orchestral Suite*, not with any conviction that he was penning a masterpiece but more as a way of keeping his hand in until something more significant came along. In fact as the autumn wore on he warmed to the task and produced a far better work than he had expected to at the start. The stay with Anatoly and Praskovya (of whom he was growing very fond – he could love a woman who was loved by his brother and so was, he thought, no threat) lasted until the middle of September. Then he made his way back to Kamenka which he knew he could not avoid any longer without being unkind to Sasha. Overlapping with this transition between brother and sister's hospitality was the composition of the *Six Piano Pieces*, Op. 51, a way of satisfying Jurgenson's need for something he could sell to make up for the 2,500 roubles Tchaikovsky had negotiated for the rights to Mazeppa. In Kamenka again for the first time in nearly a year he orchestrated the *Second Suite*, a process that was taking him ever longer as he realised that the quality and individuality of his music rested as much in his deft instrumentation as in its thematic and harmonic structure.

With *Mazeppa* in production in both St Petersburg and Moscow it was clear that for once jaunts to the club life of Paris and the street scenes of Italy would have to be foreshortened that winter. Before he left Kamenka to involve himself in the theatre he spent a few weeks after the completion of the *Second Suite* on a set of songs that were meant to be trifles but paradoxically were the most worthwhile pieces he wrote in 1883. These were the sixteen *Children's Songs*, Op. 54. The last of the set, the nonsense song, had been written in 1881 but the rest were composed at the rate of almost one a day between 28 October and 15 November 1883. Whether the idea came from Mussorgsky's *Nursery Songs*, whether it was a nostalgic response to Sasha's seven-year-old youngest boy, Yuri, or to the emerging generation of great nephews and nieces it is hard to judge. Most likely it seemed like a perfect moment to take up the suggestion of his long-standing acquaintance, Alexei Plescheyev, to set verses from his collection, *The Snowdrop*, which had been sent to Tchaikovsky two years before. This was the source for all but one of the 1883 set. It included one song – *Legend, When Jesus Christ was but a Child* – which became a minor classic in its own right. It was soon detached,

Claude Debussy (1862 - 1918), when he was twenty he played in Nadezhda von Meck's domestic piano trio.

The Industry and Art Building at the 1882 Moscow Exhibition, where the first performance of the *1812 Overture* was played.

orchestrated and set for chorus and shows Tchaikovsky at his most Russian and his most uncomplicatedly lyrical. *The Children's Songs* are charming and are meant to be but they are also among the most effective and vocally well-placed of the hundred or so songs that he wrote.

At the end of November 1883 Tchaikovsky returned from the country to Moscow, where the *First Symphony* was given a rare outing – it had not been played in public for 15 years – and gave its composer a useful chance to take stock of his progress. Time weighed on his hands during the Christmas period as the *Mazeppa* productions faced constant delays. Eventually it reached the Bolshoi stage on 15 February 1884 and the Mariinsky on 19th. On 20th the premiere of the *Second Suite* was conducted by Max Erdmannsdorfer, who had taken over the RMS concerts after Rubinstein's death.

Tchaikovsky, so often deeply sympathetic to the feelings of others, could at times be astonishingly undiplomatic and gauche in defending his own professional interests. He now made one of those *faux pas* which were entirely avoidable and quite unnecessary. He left Russia for Italy the day after *Mazeppa* was performed in Moscow and did not bother to stay for either the St Petersburg performance, conducted by Napravnik, nor for Erdmannsdorfer's concert. Since the latter was to be the first time the German had been entrusted with a new Tchaikovsky work, his irritation at the composer's nonchalance is hardly surprising. The absence from *Mazeppa* in St Petersburg was even less clever. For once the theatre had spent a generous amount of money on the production, possibly because of the new Tsar's known interest in both Tchaikovsky and the subject matter. The lavish sets and costumes had been presented to

Tchaikovsky for his approval, an unprecedented level of involvement, and great care had been taken by Jurgenson in engraving the parts and score. Tchaikovsky's escape by train meant that there was no one to receive the ovation at the Royal gala first night and the audience, including the Tsar, was left with a feeling of anti-climax. Russian society could not understand why a composer would prefer to leave the country on holiday rather than attend one of the most glittering premieres of his career. Everybody was peeved.

Tchaikovsky was soon told of his mistake and realised its seriousness. After three weeks in Paris, seeing Tanya and her son Georges-Léon (who was being fostered away from his ill mother) it was clear that he would have to go back to Russia to make peace with Napravnik. The carrot was the prospect of discussing the production details of *Evgeny Onegin*, which the Tsar had declared his favourite opera and which Napravnik was therefore to conduct the following season. On his arrival Tchaikovsky found that his favour with the Royal family was to be marked further. He had been awarded the Order of St Vladimir and was to be invested with it on 19 March in separate audiences with Alexander III and his Danish Tsarina. For Tchaikovsky, in middle-age a convinced royalist conservative, the experience was enough to send him into a state of fractured nerves which liberal mouthfuls from a bottle of bromide could do little to alleviate. The visit to the capital was a great success, however, for he found that he was not only publicly recognised as a major figure in Russian life but that *Mazeppa* was enjoying a good run at the Mariinsky.

In better humour than for some time he made the social round of Moscow before heading for Kamenka at the end of April 1884. His diary for that spring reveals his passions, irritations and working patterns. There were four occupations other than chatting with family members: walking in the woods – sometimes alone, when he noted down ideas, sometimes with his nephew Bob (now 13) – playing the card game vint most evenings, learning English (though he remained baffled by the language when he heard it spoken by the governess, Martha Eastwood) and composing. He thought about writing both another symphony and a piano concerto but could not come to grips with either and settled instead on a *Third Orchestral Suite*. He was constantly dissatisfied with the sketches but worked on steadily, finishing the piece on 6 June. He was right to be wary. The best that can be said of the *Suite* is that it is amiable and harmless. It would be less charitable but just as accurate to dismiss it as thoroughly third-rate, though competently put

Alexander III and his Danish Tsarina, Dagmar.

together. Its premiere, however, was to prove to be one of his most immediate and enthusiastic public triumphs.

Inwardly, however, Tchaikovsky was not so sanguine. When Bob arrived from school he promptly fell in love with him and the frustration this caused, because of course there was no possibility of consummating the emotion, made him irritable. The bustle of family comings and goings and the pressure of Sasha's problems confirmed the conviction, growing for some time, that he should look for a home of his own at last. He adored Sasha and her children but increasingly their troubles were being off-loaded onto him and, anxious as he was to help, he needed to put some distance between himself and the Davidov clan. He wrote to Praskovya asking her and Anatoly to keep their eyes open for a suitable property near them, outside Moscow. As his 44th birthday came and went he was feeling his age too.

After a few weeks the atmosphere at Kamenka became too much and he joined Modest at Grankino, the Konradi estate. There he orchestrated the *Third Suite* and began work on a new piece for piano and orchestra. At first he thought it would turn into a third piano concerto but a different structure of two movements appealed to him and it emerged as a *Concert Fantasia*. In August he moved to Anatoly's holiday villa where there was nursing to be done as well as work. Laroche was by now in a deplorable state, riddled with syphilis and deadened by alcohol and quite unable to summon the keen intellect which had marked him out as a young man. Tchaikovsky, relaxed after

Ivan Melnikov playing
Kochubey in the St. Petersburg
production of *Mazeppa*.

his time with Modest and confident in his new works, was for
once content to humour his friend and deal with the
professional intrigues which spilled out from nearby Moscow.
With Anatoly and Praskovya he was finding that a combination
of being in the country, where he could walk and work
uninterrupted, but still be in touch with the musical centre was
an easier pattern of life to manage than his old extremes of
Moscow, the Ukraine and abroad.

Tchaikovsky still needed to finish the *Concert Fantasia* by the
time Anatoly's lease on the house for the summer came to an
end, so he borrowed the new (and smaller) von Meck
establishment at Pleshcheyevo for September and all was duly
completed by 6 October 1884. It is not one of his strongest
inventions, though the piano writing is impressively virtuosic,
and it is almost as if Tchaikovsky was becoming too professional

147

for his own good: writing competent music in congenial surroundings that passed the time for the listener pleasantly but to no great purpose. All his music from 1884 bears this out, as if he was waiting for a new storm to release music with conflict as well as amiable flow.

With the score ready to present to Taneyev, who was to premiere it, Tchaikovsky journeyed north to St Petersburg where, at the Tsar's request, *Evgeny Onegin* was at last to be given a professional production at the Bolshoi. The first night on 31 October was the sort of moderate success that Tchaikovsky had always feared for a work which lacked fashionably spectacular scenes. Ironically the Tsar was unable to attend the opening night or several subsequent performances. However

Vera and Natalya Davidova, two of Tchaikovsky's Kamenka nieces.

the approval of the royal family ensured its future performance and within a fortnight the public was warming to it until it soon assumed the solid place in the repertoire that it has enjoyed ever since. Cui's usual diatribe had no effect and over the following seasons *Onegin* came to be not only Tchaikovsky's most popular major work but his most substantial source of income. The royal command had also ensured that the performers, especially Napravnik, treated the music with respect from the beginning and the 28-year-old soprano, Emilia Pavlovskaya (who had also taken a leading role in *Mazeppa*), scored a personal triumph as the first Tatyana.

By 1884 Balakirev had emerged from his religious isolation and had taken up his old post of Director of St Petersburg's Free Music School once again. He was back in royal favour too and his years of asceticism had earned him the post of Director of the Choir of the Imperial Chapel. For Tchaikovsky this meant both reacquaintance with his old mentor and at last the official acceptance of his church music. As he headed west for a few weeks in Berlin, Davos (where Kotek was in the later stages of consumption) and Paris after the *Onegin* production, he carried with him two commands from Balakirev. The first was for some hymns for the chapel choir, the second was to look again seriously at Byron's epic poem *Manfred* as the basis for a major orchestral work which Balakirev, in his usual thorough way, had pressed on him two years before. It had in fact been Vladimir Stasov's idea 17 years earlier and he had approached Balakirev who had in turn offered it to Berlioz (who would have suited the material rather better than Tchaikovsky).

In Davos the days Tchaikovsky spent with Kotek were painful for it was clear he was seriously ill and within a month, just after Tchaikovsky's return to St Petersburg, he was dead at the age of 30, a tragic waste of a potentially great violinist. Otherwise the periods spent in St Petersburg either side of Christmas were immensely agreeable. Modest had a new play given at the Alexandrinsky with rather more success than the last. The *Third Suite* was heard for the first time on 24 January 1885 in a concert in which von Bülow played the *First Piano Concerto* and conducted the suite to rapturous applause that stunned even the composer. In February Tchaikovsky was installed as one of the board of directors of the RMS. *Onegin* was still pulling full houses and the Tsar finally made it to the fifteenth performance. The operas generally were proving so gratifying – with *Mazeppa* and *The Maid of Orleans* joining *Onegin* during the season – that he decided to give *Vakula the Smith* a new lease of life by revising it thoroughly and retitling it

Cherevichki – a sort of high-heeled Ukrainian woman's boot – variously translated as *The Little Shoes*, *The Slippers* or *The Golden Slippers*. In view of the confusion it seems easier to refer to it here in the original Russian.

Meanwhile the determination to rent his own house that he had felt the previous spring was stiffened by an unpleasant few weeks spent with his niece, Anna, and her von Meck husband. He despatched Alyosha to cast his eye over a dacha available at Maidanovo, a mile and a half from Klin, conveniently close to the main Moscow–St Petersburg railway line. On 24 February 1885 he moved in and, though disappointed with the ugliness of

Ilya Repin's painting of the death scene from *Evgeny Onegin*.

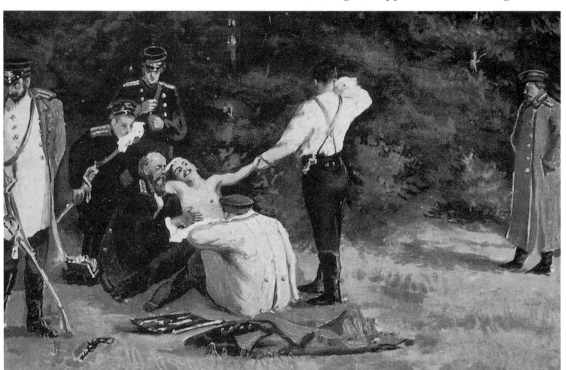

the house and the tastelessness of its decor, he soon decided it would suit him well, as he reported to Modest:

'The house is large and there will be plenty of room for all of us in summer. The surrounding countryside is charming and you will be quite satisfied. I quickly became used to the unattractive furniture, having decided that I shall not stay permanently. On the other hand the lovely view from the window, the peace and quiet, the feeling that I am in my own home, make me happy and I have been in a good humour all day... After dinner I walked to Klin along the river (a delightful walk), had tea at four o'clock and wrote a long letter to von Bülow.'

150

Chapter 10

A Home of his Own

Tchaikovsky's first work at a house that he could finally regard as home was a romantic symphony with a programme of the sort of epic proportions so typical of the nineteenth century. The hero, *Manfred*, wanders through the Alps searching for answers to life's impossible questions and the personification of his ideals. He is confronted by bucolic hunters, mountain nymphs and devilish underground spirits before glimpsing his ideal creature and dying. The story's combination of the questing metaphor, magical beings and grand scenery would have fitted Wagner, Richard Strauss, Dvořák or Liszt but it seems strangely out of place in the more refined world of Tchaikovsky. Although there are elements of all these forces in the operas (except *Onegin*) and tone poems like *Francesca da Rimini*, Shakespeare and Dante are very different spurs to the imagination than Byron. Tchaikovsky recognised this, complaining to Taneyev that he had felt trapped into writing the work by Balakirev, distrusting both his own motives for composing it and the musical philosophy involved in writing a symphony to a strict literary programme: the imposition of one artform – essentially narrative – onto another which was fundamentally expressive.

Nonetheless *Manfred* served its purpose. Tchaikovsky had not written a symphony for five years and he needed to rekindle his ability to write orchestral music with greater coherence and depth than could be accommodated in a suite. He also needed to teach himself to concentrate again after two years of writing music that never fully engaged his attention. Once settled in Maidanovo in the spring of 1885 he worked steadily on the score until September. It was a struggle and he came to resent the work because of it, veering between being convinced that it was his finest symphonic work and disliking it almost as much as he did *The Oprichnik*. Posterity has tended to agree on both counts. *Manfred* is an impressive achievement, as is Schumann's account of the same story, but it never quite rises above the over-wrought fashion of its time which – as in the paintings of the pre-Raphaelites or the poetry of Swinburne, somehow enervates the subject matter with a dose of good taste.

Tchaikovsky was not entirely isolated during 1885, nor did he confine himself totally to work on *Manfred*. He finished his transformation of *Vakula the Smith* into *Cherevichki* and arranged for its production. He allowed himself to be bullied by Jurgenson into expanding the set of hymns he had written the year before into *Nine Sacred Pieces*. Most importantly for the future of Russian music he took it upon himself, as a director of the RMS, to restore some order into the affairs of the Moscow Conservatoire which had been drifting and declining in the four years since Rubinstein's death. Neither Hubert or Karl Albrecht had shown the decisive leadership the post of director required. Tchaikovsky persuaded the board that Segei Taneyev, at only 29, should be installed and managed to convince the two warring previous directors to resume their professorial duties as well, partly at the cost of agreeing to do some teaching himself once again (though only when it suited him). In the autumn of 1885 he contributed two short pieces, a march and a chorus, to the fiftieth anniversary celebrations of his old school and his future prosperity was given a fillip by a contract from the publisher Felix Mackar for the rights of his works in France, where at last his reputation was becoming more solid.

With *Manfred* completed and despatched to Jurgenson, Tchaikovsky moved house, though still within the vicinity of

The Mariinsky Theatre, home of opera in St. Petersburg.

Klin, to smaller quarters with a two year lease where there was a better excuse for refusing casual visitors. Now that he had a bolt-hole he became more reclusive than ever, confining his rare outbursts of sociability to occasional visits to Moscow and St Petersburg. Even while *Manfred* was still being orchestrated, Tchaikovsky turned to his next opera, *Charodeyka*, usually translated as either *The Sorceress* or *The Enchantress*. His routine gave him the flexibility to deal with more than one project at a time and the mental space to concentrate without over-stretching himself. He only seemed distraught or unable to cope when in the city, where he was confronted by the demands of his fractious family or his own need for a sexual outlet.

At home the day passed with delightful monotony. He would rise just after seven, have his morning tea and read for a while before starting work at nine. He would break for lunch at exactly one, stopping even in the middle of a bar. After lunch he would go for a long walk, whatever the weather, returning at four for an hour of tea, the papers or gossip with whoever was around. From five until seven he would return to his music, then wander around the estate or play the piano until dinner. After that there would be games of vint or conversation over a drink or letters to write until he retired to his bedroom at eleven, where he would enter the day's events in his diary and read some more. His habit of dispensing sweets or coins to any local children he came across on his walks meant that they were soon far from solitary and at one point he had to give up going outside the boundaries of the estate because of the throng he had himself created. Nonetheless the generous side of Tchaikovsky's nature was hard to curtail and in February 1886 he founded, with the help of the local priest, and paid for the establishment of a school at Maidanovo for the local children who would otherwise have had a four-mile walk to any education.

It was in this atmosphere that he worked throughout the autumn of 1885 and all of 1886 on *The Sorceress*. The libretto was written for Tchaikovsky by the author of the original play, Ippolit Shpazhinsky. This meant that it had an authenticity and dramatic coherence which few of his first seven operas had enjoyed but there was the drawback that Shpazhinsky was a slow worker and the text arrived in sections while Tchaikovsky was well into the composition of the music. Nonetheless its quality impressed the composer and the steady but slow emergence of the libretto did at least stop him from over-working. So did, less satisfactorily, his social and business commitments in Moscow which, now that he was famous and within commuting distance, were constantly increasing.

Tblisi, capital of Georgia and at its centre one of the finest surviving mediaeval towns.

Max Erdmannsdorfer conducted the premiere of *Manfred* on 23 March 1886 and the complexity of the score and perhaps the fact that Tchaikovsky was now on the board meant that the RMS orchestra prepared it thoroughly and respectfully. This seemed to match the reaction of the public too: respectful and impressed. Tchaikovsky was, at nearly 46, firmly part of the establishment. St Petersburg greeted it in much the same way and even Cui (perhaps because of the Balakirev connection) was nice about the work – not entirely a good sign.

Soon after the Moscow premiere Tchaikovsky made his first trip to Georgia, a spectacular journey by carriage across the wild mountains of the Caucasus, where his brother Anatoly had been installed as Chief Prosecutor in Tblisi (then called Tiflis). It was one of the most enjoyable months for Tchaikovsky for many years for he found that his celebrity status in local society was greater than anything he had previously experienced. He was cheered and fêted at a specially arranged concert of his works put on by Mikhail Ippolitov-Ivanov, a former pupil of Rimsky-Korsakov who was almost single-handedly turning the Georgian capital into a musical centre. Only a few days later, Tchaikovsky's forty-sixth birthday was marked by a special performance of *Mazeppa* in his honour. When he left it was with tender farewells not only from family and new friends but from a crowd at the station throwing flowers into the carriage of the train.

He made for Paris but instead of the usual slog across central Europe by rail he and Alyosha took to the sea for twelve days, sailing by way of northern Turkey and Constantinople across the Mediterranean (via the erupting Mount Etna) to Marseille. Ostensibly Tchaikovsky was in Paris to sort out the adoption of his great-nephew by his childless brother, Nicholai, and to meet his new French publisher, Felix Mackar. As a result Paris was no longer the semi-anonymous haven it had been for him in the past. The Parisian musical establishment now wanted to include him and during this visit he met more French composers than he ever had before, among them Delibes (whose ballet music he especially admired), Fauré – whose *Piano Quartet* he heard and admired – Lalo and Thomas. Most affecting was his meeting with the now elderly Pauline Viardot who delighted Tchaikovsky by letting him spend an afternoon alone with the autograph score of *Don Giovanni* that she owned and which had been the opera that had first fired Tchaikovsky's love of the art form.

Once home in Maidanovo after three months he was free of social obligations and could work properly once again. *The Sorceress* progressed steadily but his emotional peace and quiet was haunted by two spectres. One was the memory of a young artillery officer who had become deeply attached to him in Tbilisi and who had shot himself only three days after Tchaikovsky left. The other was Antonina who, in one of the periods of mental instability which became more damaging and prolonged as she grew older, had started to write love letters to him again, it seems not out of any wish to extract money but out of genuine though hopeless desire.

The Sorceress was completed in draft on 30 August 1886 while Modest and Kolya Konradi had arrived at Maidanovo for a couple of weeks, and Tchaikovsky immediately embarked on fulfilling a request from the Tsarina for some more songs. He complied in double the usual measure – *Twelve Songs* which became Op. 60. This, together with intensive work on the scoring of *The Sorceress* and worries over the production of *Cherevichki*, brought on migraines and at the end of October he gave himself a break and travelled up the line to St Petersburg to spend some time with his brothers.

There he soon found himself made welcome by the second generation of the Balakirev circle, now respectful of the old sage but influenced more by the sober talent of Rimsky-Korsakov, to whom Tchaikovsky was becoming closer than he had ever been. Of the new group he was particularly impressed by Lyadov and the 21-year-old Alexander Glazunov, whose precocious musicianship was making many believe that he held the key to the future. Indeed he did but though he wrote more symphonies than any other nineteenth-century Russian and better ballet music than anyone except Tchaikovsky, it was as a teacher that he was most influential, steering the St Petersburg Conservatoire through the revolutions of 1905 and 1917 and becoming a central (if at times less than appreciated) figure in the careers of Rachmaninov, Prokofiev and Shostakovich. Glazunov's patron and mentor was Mitrofan Belayev, whose

One of the Friday night gatherings for chamber music at Belayev's house in St. Petersburg. In the front row (l. to r.) are Liadov, Stassov, Cui, Rimsky-Korsakov, Belayev and Glazunov.

fortune came from the timber business but who soon indulged his love of music by becoming the publisher for the St Petersburg composers much as Jurgenson was to those in Moscow. Belayev was generous to Tchaikovsky too, founding the Glinka Prizes, worth 500 roubles each, and awarding them on three occasions to Tchaikovsky in the 1880s.

The sunny confidence that had come over Tchaikovsky in the previous two years since he had found a place of his own and favour at court was demonstrated when – as much to his own surprise as everyone else's – he agreed to conduct the opening performances of *Cherevichki* at the Bolshoi in January 1887. Not only had he never conducted opera before, he had stood in front of an orchestra only once in the previous ten years. When he was younger the experience had filled him with uncontrollable nervous tension but now, to his amazement, the performances were a great success and he found he enjoyed himself.

'Altani [the Bolshoi's chief conductor] led me out to the orchestra whereupon the curtain immediately rose and they started presenting wreaths from the orchestra, the chorus etc. to thunderous applause. While this was going on I recovered somewhat, began the overture well and by the overture's end was already conducting with complete confidence. After the first act more wreaths were presented... I was now thoroughly composed and conducted the rest of the opera with total calm.'

The triumph and the first night party meant that Modest and Pyotr did not stagger back to bed at the von Meck house until five in the morning. Within hours the sense of joy was destroyed by a telegram telling them that their niece Tanya, who had given them so much trouble but whom they both loved despite her disastrous behaviour, had died after collapsing at a St Petersburg ball. Her abuse of morphine had brought on a heart attack at the age of 26.

In the first few months of 1887 Tchaikovsky had no time to sink into morbid reflection, however, despite the equally distressing death of Borodin and the imminence of Kondratyev's death from syphilis. *The Sorceress* was due for production and the vocal score and orchestration needed to be completed as soon as possible. Nevertheless the experience of conducting *Cherevichki* had convinced Tchaikovsky that a new and lucrative side to his career was finally in prospect and he agreed to conduct a programme of his music in St Petersburg on 17 March. If such an event was to be put together now one would expect a programme that showed the depth and seriousness of the composer's achievement. One might plan an evening (taking works written before 1887) that had *Romeo and Juliet* and the *Violin Concerto* in the first half, then a second half consisting of Tatyana's letter scene from *Onegin* and the *Fourth Symphony*. At that time, however, expectations of concert planning were very different. The evening was both longer and more fractured. Three songs, sung with piano accompaniment by Alexandra Panayeva, and solo piano pieces from Tchaikovsky's salon items were distributed among the *Second Suite*, movements from the *Serenade for Strings*, a preview of two extracts from *The Sorceress*, *Francesca da Rimini* and the *1812 Overture*. Now we would think of such a potpourri as an inept musical muddle. Then Tchaikovsky, the public and the critics (even Cui) regarded it as a huge artistic success.

Alexander Borodin (1833-1887), Perhaps he would have been an even greater composer if he had not also been one of Russia's foremost chemists and university reformers.

With *The Sorceress* finally completed and the Conservatoire exams, which Tchaikovsky found himself supervising once again, over in May, he decided to head south to see Anatoly and Praskovya, despite having to deal with the aftermath of the previous year when he and Praskovya had ensnared Ivan Verinovsky and between them precipitated his suicide. Instead of repeating his journey by land of the year before, however, Tchaikovsky took a steamer down the Volga from Nizhny-Novgorod to Baku in Azerbaijan, a two week voyage with only second-class facilities at first but one which brought him to the heart of Russia and refreshed him more than he expected after the exhausting demands of the winter.

Tchaikovsky wrote no music on the journey or during his fortnight in Tbilisi at the other end but he did make possible the building of Georgia's national opera house by writing to the Tsar a personal letter asking for state funding for the project. Confirming in his subject's mind the advantages of benevolent despotism Alexander III allocated 235,000 roubles to cover the remaining costs. Tchaikovsky then moved with Anatoly and Preskovya to the developing spa of Borzholm where, on 29 June, he set about a task very different from the high drama of opera. His perusal of the original score of *Don Giovanni* the previous year had prompted him to want to write a tribute to Mozart to coincide with the centenary of the opera's premiere. He chose four pieces – the Gigue K.574, the Minuet K.355, the *Ave Verum* and the Variations on *Unser dummer Pobel meint*, K.455 – and orchestrated them as a Suite, his fourth. The arrangements went further than simple orchestration, however. Tchaikovsky, for whom Mozart was the presiding genius of his musical taste, paid homage by transforming them into a perfect expression of the susceptibilities of his own age, turning them into gems of neo-classicism just as Stravinsky was to do 30 years later with Pergolesi in *Pulcinella*. At first Tchaikovsky resisted the title *Mozartiana* for the Suite, believing it was too close to Schumann's *Kreisleriana*, but Jurgenson persuaded him and the name has stuck.

Mozartiana was not finished in the idyllic surroundings of Borzholm but on 9 August in Aachen where Tchaikovsky had travelled in response to a telegram asking him to come to spend some last days with the dying Kondratyev. It was a request that, for the sake of all the things they had shared over 20 years of the closest friendship, he could not ignore, whatever misery it entailed. Misery it was but to his credit Tchaikovsky endured over a month of it with only a few days break to see his publisher in Paris before he was relieved by Kondratyev's nephew so that Tchaikovsky could get home in time to be at the rehearsals of *The Sorceress*. Kondratyev died on 3 October.

The visit to Paris had given Tchaikovsky the inspiration for his next work which he was keen to begin after finishing *Mozartiana*, partly to keep the compositional flow going and partly to distract him from the trying company of Kondratyev. In Paris he found time to meet up with one of his ex-students, the cellist Anatoly Brandukov, and when he returned to Aachen he wiled away the time by writing the *Pezzo Capriccioso*, a bittersweet miniature concerto which falls somewhere between *Mozartiana* and the *Violin Concerto* in mood. It is full of charm and skilful string writing and only serves to heighten the regret that Brandukov never persuaded his old teacher to produce a fully-fledged Cello Concerto, a badly needed commodity in 1887.

It was soon clear that *The Sorceress* needed cutting and he returned to Maidanovo to make the changes before final rehearsals began. For the second time in the year Tchaikovsky himself took charge of the opening night on 1 November, though Napravnik had seen to much of the musical preparation for him, and the excellence of the production as well as his own presence in the pit made it a particularly glittering occasion. He sensed that it was his own début in the city rather than the opera itself that was responsible for the enthusiasm. This was confirmed when, having remained in St Petersburg to conduct three more performances, he handed the baton over to Napravnik and the audiences immediately dropped off to half-full. He was full of disappointment and regret over two years of wasted work as he headed for Moscow.

There more conducting awaited him. On 26 November he repeated elements of his March St Petersburg programme (*Francesca*, *The 1812* and *The Sorceress* excerpts) but added to them the *Concert Fantasia* (with Taneyev as soloist) and the premiere of *Mozartiana* a month or so after the designated *Don Giovanni* anniversary. Once again the Moscow public lionised him and he retreated to Maidanovo for a three week rest before embarking on what was to be the severest test yet of his capabilities as a conductor. The prelude was the St Petersburg premiere of *Mozartiana* on 24 December. This was a curtain raiser, though, and an excuse for a drink or two with Rimsky-Korsakov, Glazunov and Lyadov who were becoming good company for some musical gossip whenever he was in the city. The real work began the next day.

The rights to most of Tchaikovsky's music in Germany and the Austrian empire were held by Daniel Rahter. Now that it was known that Tchaikovsky was willing and very able to conduct his own scores with authority and relish, Rahter combined with Mackar in Paris and the Berlin promoter Dmitri Friedrich to organise a tour of Europe. It would expose Tchaikovsky for the first time in his life to the cream of the continent's orchestras and his music to its most intense-ever examination outside Russia. On 27 December he set out for Berlin and his preliminary meeting with Friedrich to prepare the details of the coming months of touring. It was not a perfect match. Friedrich badly misjudged the temperament and personality of his new star and tried to throw him into a hectic round of public functions and appearances. Tchaikovsky resisted and by the time he arrived in Leipzig for his first concerts with the Gewandhaus Orchestra he would have happily given up the whole idea had not Adolph Brodsky, who had done so much to champion the *Violin Concerto*, taken him in hand. The day after his arrival he found himself at Brodsky's house in one of those gatherings which any music lover would have paid a great deal to attend. Tchaikovsky discovered Brodsky practising chamber music with Brahms and they were joined a little later by Grieg and his wife. Of his fellow composers Tchaikovsky greatly preferred the latter. Brahms's music left him cold and irritated and he thought his reputation out of proportion to his talent. The premiere of the *Double*

The poster for Tchaikovsky's performance of his First Orchestral Suite in the Leipzig Geawandhaus, 5 January 1888. Fanny Davies, who played Beethoven in the second half, was born in Guernsey, studied with Clara Schumann and later in life often accompanied Pablo Casals.

160

Ethel Smyth, Tchaikovsky's fellow homosexual composer. He was rather more impressed by her than by her dog and her admiration for the music of Brahms.

Concerto, which he heard given during the stay, did nothing to change his opinion and, although the two men became convivial drinking companions, there was always an element of wary incomprehension between them. With Grieg, though, the relationship was immediately warm.

Tchaikovsky's first rehearsal with the Gewandhaus Orchestra – of the *First Suite* – was scheduled for 2 January 1888 and it was a nerve-wracking experience, not helped by having Brahms in the hall listening. The orchestra soon showed its approval, though, and the second rehearsal, with a paying audience including Grieg, augured well for the concert itself. The night before he met the formidable English composer

Ethel Smyth, the first woman composer of distinction he had come across, complete with her dog, a shambolically-behaved red setter. These two great homosexual musicians responded to each other with amused bafflement. Tchaikovsky remembered that,

'Since no Englishwoman is without her originalities and eccentricities, Miss Smyth has hers which are: firstly, the superb dog, which is quite inseparable from this lonely woman and invariably announced her arrival, not only on this occasion but at other times when I met her; secondly, a passion for hunting, on account of which Miss Smyth occasionally returns to England; and thirdly, an incredible and almost passionate worship for the enigmatic musical genius of Brahms.'

Ethel Smyth's recollections were almost the mirror image,

'Between [Tchaikovsky] and myself a relation now sprang up that surely would have ripened into close friendship had circumstances favoured us; so large minded was he that I think he would have put up unresentingly with all I had to give his work – a very relative admiration. Accustomed to the uncouth, almost brutal manners affected by many German musicians as part of the make up and one of the symptoms of genius, it was a relief to find in this Russian, who even the rough diamonds allowed was a master on his own lines, a polished cultivated gentleman and man of the world. Even his detestation of Brahms's music failed to check my sympathy – and that I think is strong testimony to his charm!'

Antonin Dvořák (1841-1904), only a few months older than Tchaikovsky, their international careers were developing in parallel.

The Leipzig orchestral concert was a critical and public success which was repeated the following day by one of his chamber music, including the *Piano Trio* and *First String Quartet*. He left for Berlin and more negotiations over the planned appearance at the Philharmonic before relaxing for a few days in Lübeck. There he received news that the Tsar, prompted by Tchaikovsky's long-term supporter as Director of the Imperial Theatres, Ivan Vsevolozhsky, had secured part of his finances in future by granting him a life-long annual subsidy of 3,000 roubles.

From Lübeck he moved on to Hamburg, where Vasily Sapelnikov (to whom he was immediately attracted) joined him to play the *First Piano Concerto*. The reaction in the press to what was in effect a three-day festival of Tchaikovsky's music was respectful and well researched in a way the more partisan critics in Russia – nominally his friends – rarely were. Although

Paris in about 1890. Long Tchaikovsky's favourite city, he took full advantage of its relaxed attitude to sex and the variety of its musical and theatrical life.

not uniformly raving, the reviews had a sincerity which he found gave him more believable support than unqualified praise would have done. There was then a two-week break before his appearance with the newly-formed Berlin Philharmonic and he rejoined the Brodsky household in Leipzig, where he added Mahler and Busoni to his list of composers encountered and saw more of Smyth and Grieg.

The latter travelled specially to Berlin for his new friend's concert, devoted entirely to Tchaikovsky's music and including the *First Piano Concerto* again (though this time with Alexander Siloti as soloist) and the *1812 Overture*, which seemed to appeal to the military tastes of the Prussians. From Berlin Tchaikovsky had his first experience of the telephone when he called Brodsky in Leipzig. The new invention was not yet a domestic convenience and a call involved both parties being available in a telephone office for a booked call. Tchaikovsky was so nervous of the experience he had to give up talking after only a moment or two. He was now a thoroughly fêted public figure, as he discovered when he returned to Leipzig and was serenaded by a military band playing God Save the Tsar and a selection of his works outside his window early one morning.

While German reaction to his appearance had been warmer than he had seriously expected it to be, his arrival in the Bohemian capital, Prague, became an excuse for a public

St. James's Hall, where Tchaikovsky gave his London concerts, stood on Piccadilly. It was opened in 1858 and seated 2,500.

outpouring so extreme it bordered on political insurrection. There were echoes of the Italian reaction to Verdi 40 years earlier. In Prague the Czech people revered him as a great Slav artist, an embodiment of their determination to be free of the Austro-Hungarian empire, just as, a hundred years later, they were to be equally eager to be free of the Russian empire. From the border he was given official protection and was met at the station in Prague by a cheering throng. He met Dvořák on his first evening (at a performance of Verdi's *Otello*). The two became firm friends and before Tchaikovsky left Prague Dvořák presented him with the manuscript of his *Symphony in D minor*. At concerts and balls given in his honour it was made clear that he was regarded as much more than a visiting musician. Tchaikovsky was seen as an agent of Slav recognition by the international community. His first concert included the works that had made up the German programmes with the addition of the *Violin Concerto* (with Karel Halir as soloist) and *Romeo and Juliet*. Two days later in the National Theatre he repeated the *1812 Overture* and watched the first performance outside Russia of Act II of *Swan Lake*, an occasion which moved him more than all the rest. For the future he was even more delighted when, at the celebratory banquet, it was agreed with Frantisek Subert that he should return later in the year to conduct *Evgeny Onegin*, the opera he was convinced was too unconventional to be staged professionally outside Russia.

A less than flattering review in the *Musical Times* for Tchaikovsky's first London concert, lamenting that he did not conduct anything more substantial than the *Serenade* for strings.

native land), came over to London and conducted their performance. M. Tschaikowsky, as amateurs well know, is the author of a large number of important works, although he devoted himself to music somewhat late. For the best of these we might naturally have looked under the circumstances of his *début* in England; but, for some reason or other, the composer preferred to bring a Serenade in four movements for strings, and a theme with variations taken from a Suite in G major, of which it is the *Finale*. He caused these to be performed in Paris as well as London, from which it may be inferred that they are specially representative. Value of some kind they undoubtedly have. The Serenade comprises an interesting Allegro in sonatina form; a very pretty Waltz, an Adagio full of earnest and expressive elegiac strains, and a *Finale* constructed upon a rollicking and simple Russian air. All the movements are distinguished by skilful workmanship and the faculty of turning the means employed to full account. As much may be said of the Suite movement, laid out for a large orchestra, from which contrasted groups of instruments are taken for use in the variations, and employed with good effect. But while recognising the merits of M. Tschaikowsky's selections, we venture to hope that they are not the best works in his catalogue. Amateurs would have preferred music of greater pretence, and in character adapted to allow a comparison between the Russian master and his contemporaries on the ground of the highest art. The Philharmonic audience, however, did not permit any consideration of this sort to affect the cordiality with which they received M. Tschaikowsky, or their sympathetic attitude towards the works actually presented. Both composer and works were applauded far beyond the limit of merely courteous approbation. The fourth novelty was Svendsen's second Norwegian Rhapsody—an interesting piece, slight in texture, but sonorous and animated. Among other pieces in the programme were Mendelssohn's Violin Concerto, finely and sympathetically played by M. Ondricek, and two songs contributed in a satisfactory manner by Miss Eleanor Rees.

LONDON SYMPHONY CONCERTS.

We have now to chronicle the two final performances of Mr. Henschel's enterprise, which took place on Wednesday afternoon, February 29, and Tuesday evening, the 6th ult. On the former occasion there was an excellent audience, Beethoven's Pastoral Symphony being probably the main attraction. So far as regards orchestral works, the ultra-conservatism of the public is as marked as ever. Liszt's extraordinary "Todtentanz" for pianoforte and orchestra was repeated, probably at the request of the Princess of Wales, who arrived during the performance of Mendelssohn's

Allegretto which does all played, but with this exc fairly good, and Mr. Cov form at the close. The was Liszt's Symphonic Poer which had only been pe London—namely, at one of nearly fifteen years ago. surprising, for, on the whole musicians generally than so "Tasso" of course belongs was composed as a kind of the same subject, which centenary of the German po Liszt in his work, the inn best understood by quoting have called up the great s to-day, haunting the lagu caught a glimpse of his fi among the *fêtes* of Ferrara, pieces; lastly, we have eternal city, which crov the martyr and the poet." to a large extent upon a gondoliers to the stroph theme enters extensively first movement or "Lame point to the graceful walt: Ferrara rejoicings. Both t structing the principal subj so that a spirit of uni greatly to its advantage. the "Tasso" had been he not be allowed to slum Wagner's Siegfried's Tod, the Concert to an early co the pecuniary loss has been first season, and on the st fund has been obtained, a arranged for next winter, and two morning Concerts. in some instances be consid the hope is expressed tha larger amount of support, b

MONDAY AND SATURI

In order to complete our is necessary to go back as February 25. This, howe formal notice, as the prog equally familiar. Schumar

The carnival moved on to Paris where Mackar made sure that his reception, while less emotional, was not an anti-climax after Bohemia. Tchaikovsky began by conducting a concert billed as private but in fact involving the Colonne Orchestra from the Châtelet and the premiere of the *Pezzo Capriccioso* (with its begetter Brandukov) to an audience of 300 of Paris's most glittering society on 28 February 1888. The two public events were shared with Colonne at the Châtelet in the first week of March. The largest scale works included were the *Concert Fantasia*, *Francesca da Rimini* and the *Violin Concerto*. The English writer, William Apthorp, described the conductor:

'Tchaikovsky's appearance at the head of an orchestra was striking. Tall and slim of figure, with short, thick iron-grey hair, moustache, and imperial, there was something military in his bearing, in the grave, dignified response he bowed to his reception from the audience... His beat in conducting was unostentatious, he used his left arm but little. But his down-beat was admirably clear and precise and, whenever he gave the signal for the thunder to break loose, the whole orchestra seemed to shiver.'

Oddly – and inaccurately – the press accused Tchaikovsky of being German-influenced, a charge that those in Prague or Leipzig would have regarded as perfectly incredible. However, Paris has always had a bizarre view of anything that is not ostentatiously Parisian. Outside the concerts Tchaikovsky added to his impressive acquaintance with musicians of his own age when he met Gounod, Paderewski, Widor and Massenet as well as renewing his friendship with Viardot and Fauré. To Modest, Tchaikovsky gave a breathless account of the social round:

'Gounod loudly demonstrated his admiration at the concert and all the young musicians are also very friendly. I have met practically everybody; Delibes is the most pleasant of all. The papers are much occupied with me and I have had a series of interviews with various journalists. One of them wrote an especially nice article about me in *Les Temps*. Next Wednesday there will be a big reception given by *Le Figaro*... I dined twice with Princess Orussova and Widor gave me a huge lunch... I return to the hotel completely exhausted and flop down to sleep like a log.'

The wonderful round of receptions, interviews, toasts and dinners would have seemed rather more genuine, however, if Tchaikovsky had been paid for his conducting. Instead it seems Mackar and Colonne had hatched a convenient scheme whereby the composer took part in the concerts entirely as a promotional exercise. Mackar reaped the profits through sales and Colonne kept the Châtelet ticket money. Tchaikovsky was expected to fend for himself.

It was in this spirit that he refused further conducting offers in France and Belgium that year and crossed the Channel to England, where at least the Royal Philharmonic Society in London proposed to pay him for his work. The fee was not large – £20, which his agent, Francesco Berger, managed to have increased to £25 on the strength of the concert's success – but it was better than nothing. The journey itself was trying, however:

'Last night I left Paris in a frightful snowstorm. The crossing was awful!!! I was the only one who was not sick. I am quite certain now that I do not get seasick. I reached London at midnight instead of seven o'clock and there is deep snow everywhere as with us in January.'

Once installed at the Hotel Dieudonné life felt better. The Hotel was a haven of France in London. It only boasted 16 rooms (and only one bathroom) but its chef was famous and to be invited to join the table d'hôte was an honour not always granted. Those that did had to sign their names on the wall and, if they were artists, embellish the autograph with a fragment of their work. It is one of the tragedies of London's history that this wall was demolished when the building changed hands, for among those who used Dieudonné's as their base were Rubinstein, Rodin, Whistler, Saint-Saëns, George Moore, Sargent, Massenet and Sickert as well as Edward, Prince of Wales. For the musicians it had the added advantage of being in Ryder Street, only a short stroll from St James's Hall, London's main concert venue, on the north side of Piccadilly where the Piccadilly Hotel is today (to make way for which this historic hall was destroyed; another act of cultural vandalism, though its acoustics could not compare with the Châtelet or the Gewandhaus on which it was modelled).

The programme for Tchaikovsky's first London appearance was not taxing – the *Serenade for Strings* and the *Variations from the Third Orchestral Suite* – and the rest of the evening was similarly light. Frederic Cowan conducted works by Ernst, Svendsen, a Haydn symphony and accompanied Frantisek Ondricek in Mendelessohn's *E minor violin concerto*. Cowan recalled that, 'he did not speak English and I had to stand at his side all the time and translate his wishes to the members of the orchestra.' In fact Tchaikovsky had struggled to learn English for years and though he could read it tolerably well, never felt confident in his ability to pronounce it properly. Away from the concert hall Tchaikovsky occupied his time with recuperating at the hotel and visiting a peculiar ballet called *The Sports of England* (which bored him) at the Empire Leicester Square and a visiting French company's production of Molière's *Tartuffe* in Soho. At the Empire he missed the point, which was not to see the ballet but to encounter London's highest-class prostitutes who wandered elegantly in the Promenade.

London was the last engagement of the tour and he left on

24 March by train to join Anatoly in Tbilisi. It was a long, tiring journey, broken by a two-day stop in Vienna and a few days visiting his brother Ippolit (with whom he was beginning to lose touch) at Taganrog on the Sea of Azov. Other than going to Kamenka there was little choice, since he had relinquished the lease on Maidanovo and Alyosha had not yet found a new house to suit them. He remained in Georgia for just under a month before a new home was now ready at Frolovskoye, still in the vicinity of Klin. He was anxious after so many months of train journeys to settle somewhere he could call home and resume serious composition. He arrived on 3 May 1888 and was delighted with his servant's choice. Frolovskoye was to be the catalyst for his most important burst of composition of the decade.

The house Tchaikovsky rented at Frolovskoe in the spring of 1888, ugly but with plenty of room.

Chapter 11

Fame but Small Fortune

By 1888 Tchaikovsky had not written a symphony without a literary programme for eleven years. Despite the supply and relative success of his operas in Russia and the popularity of his various concert pieces, it was clear that if he wanted to be accepted as a major figure in the German-influenced music world, a solid base of symphonic achievement was needed and his earlier attempts were too nationalistic to fit the bill. This seems to have been what the octogenarian chairman of the Hamburg Philharmonic, Theodor Avé-Lallement, had told him firmly when they met (the old man went too far in demanding that Tchaikovsky also settle in Germany if he wanted to make anything of himself). Once back in Frolovskoye Tchaikovsky decided to take the advice. Dvořák, whose reputation, like Tchaikovsky's, also rested on a combination of opera, symphonies, national tone poems, chamber music and songs, may have influenced the decision too.

At first the composition was hard and Tchaikovsky struggled. Given the length of time since he had written seriously it was hardly surprising but he fretted that there was nothing left to say. Gradually though the atmosphere of the new surroundings, the high-roomed house, the fine garden, the direct walk into the woods and the isolation of the holiday dacha suburbia of Maidanovo, settled him down. The domestic arrangements were calmer too. Alyosha had long passed the age when Tchaikovsky found him attractive and he had married while his master was abroad. *The Fifth Symphony* was begun in June 1888 and the sketches were done by the end of the month. Increasingly, though, the real work for Tchaikovsky was in the orchestration rather than in the original melodic and harmonic material. This was clear from the fact that immediately the Symphony was drafted he moved on to rough out a *Fantasy Overture on Hamlet*, which he accomplished in under a week, before returning to work on the instrumental allocation of the Symphony. This process took him until the end of August, when

The garden at the back of the house at Frolovskoe.

he despatched the score to Taneyev, who was to make the regulation arrangement for piano duet that publishers relied upon for their sales.

The contrast between the *Fifth Symphony* and the *Hamlet* Fantasy could not be more striking and shows how careful the critic has to be in applying biographical motives for music. While the Symphony is a mature balance between drama and a mellow serenity – with its extraordinary slow movement horn solo introducing us to a very different view of love from his works of the 1870s – clearly designed for the western establishment, *Hamlet* is a tight essay on psychological desperation. The Symphony was dedicated, in a surprising but politically astute gesture, to Avé-Lallement, *Hamlet* to Grieg. Oddly, he seems to have had no further contact with either of them.

Tchaikovsky's self-confidence can be gauged not only from the music of the two new works but from the fact that he was prepared to conduct the premieres in St Petersburg himself, a prospect which would have flattened him a few years earlier. There were other ghosts being laid too, for in October 1888 he composed the *Six French Songs, Op. 65*, for Désirée Artôt. They had met again the previous year in Berlin, having not seen each other since she had run off with her Spanish tenor 20 years before. Now Artôt was in her early fifties and coming to the end of her career but she asked her old admirer for a song. He responded with a full set, to her delight and astonishment and when he returned to Berlin in the winter she was a close companion once again. Other personal commitments during the autumn were a mixture of pleasure and pain. He orchestrated an overture for his old friend Laroche (who had been in residence for much of the summer) and visited the family at Kamenka, where learned that Sasha was no better and that his niece Vera was dying of TB in France.

Because Tchaikovsky was prepared to direct his major works himself, premieres now had an interest far greater than in the past. So the *Fifth Symphony's* first performance (along with that of the Laroche *Karmozina* Overture) on 17 November was followed by a second the following week which added *Hamlet* to the repertoire. From St Petersburg he hurried to Prague, conducting the foreign premiere there of the *Fifth Symphony* on 30 November (to a small house but Tchaikovsky scored a diplomatic triumph by donating his share of the proceeds to the Musicians' pension fund) and of *Evgeny Onegin* on 6 December. Frantisek Subert left an evocative memoir of that performance, particularly of Tchaikovsky's lack of theatrical experience:

'Not very accustomed to it, he directed his attention chiefly to the orchestra without concerning himself much with the stage. To forestall any unwelcome shipwreck at the premiere the first conductor [of the National Theatre] sat in the prompt box and co-operated in the performance exactly as Italian operatic prompters do, who not only prompt but also give the singers the beat and all other necessary directions... At rehearsals, and especially at the performance, the composer was very excited and as a keen smoker went out after every scene to smoke a cigarette... According to the theatre's internal regulations it was strictly forbidden. But because Tchaikovsky as a smoker was uncontrollable, everyone turned a blind eye when he took refuge in the conductor's room near the orchestra. There, by an open window in December... he rolled his cigarettes and lit up, drinking mineral water with cognac.'

He returned immediately to Russia, pausing for family business in St Petersburg before going on to Moscow to conduct what was now becoming a touring programme of the *Fifth Symphony* and the *Second Piano Concerto* (with Sapelnikov) on 22 December.

At home in Frolovskoye after Christmas Tchaikovsky set to work on a new ballet. He had a month before he was required to set out on his next conducting tour and he made the most of

An early picture of Marius Petipa (1818-1910) who, as Imperial Ballet Master, dominated 19th-century Russian dance. He was in late middle age by the time he choreographed Tchaikovsky's great ballets.

it, producing the sketch of a score which has remained one of his most enduring successes. Earlier in the year Ivan Vsevolozshky, the director of the Imperial Theatres and one of his most faithful supporters, had suggested using a fairy tale by the eighteenth-century French writer, Charles Perrault, as the core of a full evening of dance. The tale agreed on was *The Sleeping Beauty*, which Tchaikovsky had told to Sasha's children nearly 20 years before. Conditions at the ballet were very different from the inadequate days of *Swan Lake*. Marius Petipa, the chief choreographer at the Mariinsky since 1869, had gradually built the company into the finest ballet troupe in the world, a position it has held (in the Soviet era as the Kirov) with only occasional lapses ever since. Petipa produced a detailed scenario and delivered it to Tchaikovsky during the autumn so that by January 1889 the composer had all the materials he needed.

After a quick progress report to Vsevolozhsky and Petipa in St Petersburg he set off to conduct in Germany on 5 February 1889. After a few preparatory days in Berlin he gave the first concert in Cologne on the 12th and the second in Frankfurt three days later (the *Third Orchestral Suite* was his only commitment). On the 20th he offered Dresden the *Fourth Symphony* and the *First Piano Concerto* but the players were less able to cope than in other cities and although the press reception was euphoric, Tchaikovsky was livid and homesick when he returned to Berlin the next day. Despite this, Artôt took her old friend in hand and the rehearsals with the Berlin Philharmonic went well. At the concert on 26 February, though, there were hisses among the cheers for *Francesca da Rimini* and Tchaikovsky, hypersensitive to anything except adulation, left Berlin in an even fouler mood than he had arrived. He paused in Leipzig for two days of soothing by Adolph Brodsky and his wife before taking the train to Geneva for the next event. An unexpected triumph there, with an orchestra that he had at first feared was too small and ill-prepared for the *First Suite* and the *Serenade for Strings*, set him back on course, though his memories of days by the lake with Modest and Kotek brought on a fit of tearful nostalgia. Geneva had been something of a detour since he had then to make his way north again to Hamburg for a final German appearance on 15 March. There he was flattered to find that Brahms had not only stayed in the city especially to hear the *Fifth Symphony*, he was lodged in the next room in the hotel. They were always doubtful of each other's music but the personal respect was deep and since Brahms's judgement on the symphony was that he liked

Johannes Brahms (1833-1897). He and Tchaikovsky liked each other well enough but were never quite convinced they liked each other's music.

everything except the last movement – a view Tchaikovsky had come to share – there was enough common ground for them to go and get pleasantly drunk together over lunch after the rehearsal.

The final concert of the spring had been fixed for London but it was a month away and Tchaikovsky, rather than go home, decided to relax for the early spring in Paris at the Hotel Richepense, without at first making any professional announcement that he was in the city. Instead he dallied with *The Sleeping Beauty*, enjoyed the café life and indulged in the sexual license that Paris on the verge of the naughty Nineties afforded, whatever one's inclination. Word that he was in town soon leaked out, of course, and he attended the Châtelet to hear Colonne conduct the *Third Suite*, spent time with Viardot, Fauré, the cellist Brandukov and made friends with Massenet before Sapelnikov (to whom he was fiercely attracted) joined him for the trip to London.

The Philharmonic Society there had originally wanted to commission a symphony from him (as it had done from Beethoven and Dvořák) but Tchaikovsky explained that he had just completed the Fifth and was reluctant to begin another so soon. The Society then offered to present that but the composer, in a combination of failure of nerve and the wish to give Sapelnikov a memorable début, professed himself unhappy with the symphony's orchestration and pressed the society to accept the *First Orchestral Suite* and *Piano Concerto* instead. Sapelnikov and Tchaikovsky arrived on 9 April and were amazed the next morning to find that the infamous London pea soup fog made it almost impossible to find their way from the rehearsal in Piccadilly back to Ryder Street. Not surprisingly, since he had only ever been to London in bad weather, he was beginning to dislike the city heartily. It had not helped that the rehearsal had been a bad-tempered affair, solely because Frederic Cowan and himself had to share the conducting of the two-hour concert and neither had enough time to prepare the orchestra properly. As usual the management was relying on the famed sight-reading abilities of London players to save the day, which they did but to nobody's satisfaction. Sapelnikov, however, scored a triumph on 11 April as Tchaikovsky had hoped (in one review his own appearance was not even mentioned, much to his fury), and soon became a regular fixture of the London concert scene.

The previous year's journey from London to Tbilisi was repeated, starting the morning after the St James's Hall concert. Rather than subject himself to the interminable train again, though, he crossed France to Marseille and boarded a steamer for Batum on the Black Sea. The voyage lasted for eleven days, during which he endured gales and revelled in the company of two teenage Russian boys. He was too tired to enjoy the trip properly or to do more than tinker with *The Sleeping Beauty* and when he arrived in Georgia (where Anatoly was now deputy governor of the area) he found that his brother and Praskovya had arranged a hectic social round to celebrate his stay.

There was little respite when he arrived back in Moscow at the beginning of May, either. As a director of the RMS and now something of a father figure to the Moscow Conservatoire he had to mediate over the resignation of its director for the third time since Nicholai Rubinstein's death. This time it was Sergei Taneyev who had had enough of the internal politics. Replacing him with Vasily Safonov proved to be a time-consuming and messy process of the sort that Tchaikovsky was remarkably efficient at sorting out but which he resented as a waste of energy. Alongside the responsibilities as an RMS director there were exams to supervise, details of the following season's concerts to arrange (Tchaikovsky had been busy distributing invitations to conduct on his travels, to Dvořák among others) and, in St Petersburg, more meetings with Petipa.

It was the last day of May 1889 before he was able to return to Frolovskoye after four months and immerse himself in *The Sleeping Beauty*, which had to be ready by September. In his diary he noted that he finished the sketches on 7 June at 8pm: 'In all I worked ten days in October, three weeks in January, and now a week: so, in all, about forty days.' After a few days' rest he began to score the ballet, taking far greater care over the task than he had often in the past but admitting to Nadezhda von Meck that, while he was frightened it signified a decline in his inventiveness, it was not a bad development. 'I have devised several completely new orchestral combinations which I hope will be very beautiful and interesting.' He was right and the use of wind and piano can be seen as a gentle precursor of the next century, while the lightness of touch he brings to the instrumental colouring shows the influence of his love of Paris and his liking for Delibes and Fauré. Laroche hit the nail on the head when he reviewed that 'it has a French tint to it but it smells of Russia.' The work was finished on time on 28 August and dedicated to its commissioner, Ivan Vsevolozshky.

The first half of September was spent at Kamenka, where he found Sasha much more her normal self than she had been the previous year and where he recognised the growing importance in his life of his nephew Bob. Whether he realised at this stage

The programme for the Philharmonic Society's concert on 11 April 1889. Tchaikovsky is placed either side of the interval. Following him with Handel and Purcell songs would never be countenanced now but probably worked better than the overture by Vincent Wallace.

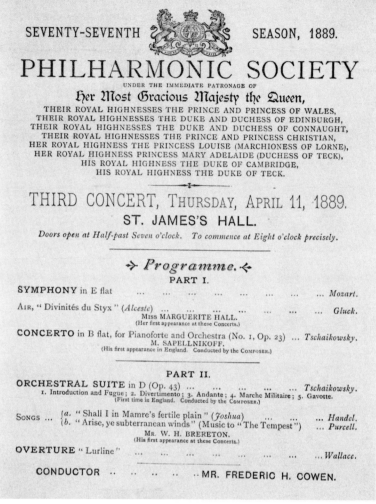

that they shared much the same sexual tastes is not clear, though it would be remarkable if he did not. Either way the infatuation was strong enough to make him consider moving to St Petersburg again to be near the youth.

After the sojourn in Ukraine he spent the rest of the autumn in an exhausting round of conducting engagements, shuttling back and forth between Moscow and St Petersburg. At the Bolshoi he conducted a new production of *Onegin* and at the Mariinsky he was on hand to rehearse *The Sleeping Beauty*. Of equal significance, though, was the fact that he was now conducting other people's music too. The celebrations surrounding Anton Rubinstein's 50 years in the profession and Tchaikovsky's duties to the Moscow RMS (after Erdmannsdorfer's departure) needed him to be more active. As part of these he conducted Beethoven's *Ninth Symphony* and

Rubinstein's *The Tower of Babel* which required 800 musicians – a number comparable with even the grandest performances of Berlioz' *Requiem* or Mahler's *Eighth Symphony*. Tchaikovsky handled all this with patience and skill and from among his own works conducted the *Violin Concerto*, the *Fifth Symphony*, *Pezzo Capriccioso*, *Hamlet*, the *First Piano Concerto* and the *Concert Fantasia*. Despite this clear indication of his pre-eminent position in Russian music (recognised by Chekhov, who that month dedicated a volume of short stories to him and wrote to Modest that he was second only to Tolstoy as a Russian artist) Tchaikovsky was still shocked by Anton Rubinstein's childish humiliation of him at the dinner after the *Tower of Babel* concert when he pointedly accused Tchaikovsky of having no love for him but only for his brother Nicholai who had died eight years earlier. Nonetheless relations with his old teacher were still warm enough for him to conduct the premiere of Rubinstein's *Konzertstuk* for piano and orchestra with Rubinstein performing as soloist. He was hurt too when the premiere of *The Sleeping Beauty*, which he decided was his best work since *Onegin*, met with only cool approval from the Tsar and the first night audience at the Mariinsky on 15 January 1890.

Fed up and exhausted, he decided to leave Russia for the winter and headed for Florence where, for once, he knew nobody. With him travelled Nazar Litrov, Modest's young servant, for Alyosha no longer went abroad with Tchaikovsky and on this occasion needed to remain in Frolovskoye to nurse his sick wife, Fekla. Within a month she too had been killed by tuberculosis. In Florence Tchaikovsky took rooms at the Hotel Washington on the banks of the River Arno and established his writing routine. After a year of light ballet music he had been preparing through the autumn to tackle a more demanding work: his first opera since *The Sorceress* in 1886. For a libretto he turned to two familiar sources, his brother Modest and Pushkin. Modest was beginning to have mild success as a playwright of sentimental drama and he set about turning Pushkin's ironic 1834 short story *The Queen of Spades* (known in France as *Pique Dame*) into tragic opera.

In Florence Tchaikovsky found his regular life of writing and walking was as easy to maintain as it was in Frolovskoye. In the city he soon felt lonely and bored, however, and Florence soon felt desperately claustrophobic. Nonetheless the opera progressed with a perfect rhythm so that in eight weeks the task of composing the short score was done. Vsevolozshky had commissioned the work for production the following autumn so Tchaikovsky's speed was for once a matter of deadline rather

Anton Rubinstein. As a pianist he was more influential internationally than as a composer. Despite Tchaikovsky's involvement in the celebrations for his 50 years in the profession, Rubinstein found it hard to be generous to his most famous pupil.

than inspiration. The popular image of Tchaikovsky as a romantic figure writing only in the white heat of emotional confession is thoroughly wide of the mark. He was one of the most conscientious and professional musicians of his generation and certainly the most workmanlike of Russian composers, equalled in diligence only by Rimsky-Korsakov.

He left Florence with a sigh of relief on 7 April, two days after finishing the draft of *The Queen of Spades* and spending time in the Uffizi gallery and Pitti Palace where he admitted that he remained quite unmoved by the glories of Renaissance art, enjoying only the portraits. Arriving in Rome he immediately wished he had decided to spend the winter there instead, though he realised he would probably have found maintaining the discipline needed for composition more difficult. This was even more apparent when his old playmate

Prince Golitsyn appeared and involved him in the social round. Orchestrating *The Queen of Spades* had to take priority, though, and by the end of the month, the work half done, he had had enough of Italy and journeyed back to St Petersburg in time to mark his fiftieth birthday quietly with Modest (whose own fortieth fell six days later).

He visited Moscow to see Jurgenson but also to follow up his resignation letter from the RMS board. He had clashed with Vasily Safonov, whom he had worked so hard to install peacefully as head of the Conservatoire. On Fitzhagan's death in March Tchaikovsky had pressed hard for the professorship of cello to be given to Brandukov. Safonov refused and Tchaikovsky felt that his musical judgement was likely to be called into question increasingly by the over-ambitious director. Not only did Tchaikovsky relinquish his place on the board, he pulled out of conducting six concerts the following autumn – a major part of the season – and the intrigue left a bitter taste.

It was to be the predominant feeling of the summer. At Frolovskoye he found the woods at the end of the garden, which had been his main delight, had been felled by the new landlord, leaving him only desolate open country to walk across. He

Tchaikovsky found Florence beautiful but dull. It was good for getting opera written in peace, though.

thought of going back to Maidanovo but found all the villas booked and even considered spending summer in the city in St Petersburg, a real sign of desperation. In the end he grumbled, stayed at Frolovskoye and finished off the orchestration of *The Queen of Spades*.

As so often with Tchaikovsky, once the creative flame was burning he could not merely snuff it out at the end of a work but had to find more fuel for it immediately. Within a week of completing the opera he picked up an idea which had been floating around since 1887 – a sextet for strings, the fulfilment of a promise to write something for the St Petersburg Chamber Music Society. Some of the thematic material had come to him during the winter and, unsuitable for the opera, had been put

The lake in the grounds of Frolovskoe.

to one side. While the melodic material flowed easily enough he found the form harder to contain after two months thinking in terms of a large orchestra but the sextet was still written at the rate of one movement per week. It was complete in draft by 12 July and subtitled *Souvenir de Florence*, an epithet that referred more to the place itself than to any lingering love the composer felt for it. The score was ready for the copyist on 6 August 1890 (though it was substantially revised the following year after discussions with Glazunov).

As in the previous two years the late summer was to be spent visiting family around the southern reaches of the empire. With the conducting engagements of the autumn cancelled, however, there was time for a much more extended trip and, after a happy week at Grankino with Modest and Bob, he collected Kolya Konradi and moved on to Kamenka. There

179

Sasha was now clearly falling apart, ravaged by morphine and alcohol. Thoroughly depressed by his sister's state he and Kolya journeyed south to Tblisi where, instead of joining Anatoly's household, they rented an apartment. In this state of sociable independence Tchaikovsky turned again to Pushkin, this time for the structure of a symphonic poem. Confusingly his choice had the same title as the play by Ostrovsky he had used for first opera, *The Voyevoda*. In the days before recordings, however, the clash can have hardly mattered to the composer who little expected his apprentice work ever to surface again. It was while he was working on the new *Voyevoda* that he received a letter which knocked his self-confidence more than almost any he had received and did much to embitter his remaining years.

Souvenir de Florence, the autograph score of the string sextet.

Chapter 12

An End Too Soon

The letter that arrived at Tchaikovsky's flat in Tblisi on 4 October 1890 is one of the few from Nadezhda von Meck not to have survived. It is quite likely that it was the one he least wanted to keep. From subsequent events, and his immediate reply, we do know roughly what it said, however. She was worn

The Tchaikovsky brothers together in 1890. From l. to. r. Anatoly, Nicholai, Ippolit, Pyotr and Modest.

down by disaster and she could no longer afford to give him an allowance, therefore she assumed there was little point in further contact. In fact matters were not quite as bad as she thought but there was plenty to worry about. Her own fortune was based on the railways which her husband had built. The Government was gradually bringing these under state control and so the income was drying up. At the same time her children were proving to be hopeless at business, mismanaging the family estates and losing large proportions of their inheritance in fruitless speculative ventures. Her own health, physical and mental, was deteriorating badly. She was becoming a lonely old woman convinced that her money was the only reason she had friends and that without it there was nothing. In breaking off with Tchaikovsky she would have had the support of her long-time secretary and recent son-in-law, Wladislav Pachulski, a failed composer who had never forgiven Tchaikovsky for being honest about his meagre talent. Had she and Tchaikovsky had a normal relationship they perhaps would have been able to meet and talk through the crisis. But neither was able to be that open. Tchaikovsky was distraught, not because of the money so much – he admitted that the cut in his income would hurt but was only telling the truth when he wrote that 'in recent years my income has greatly increased and there is no reason to doubt that it will continually and rapidly grow' – but because she closed her letter, it seems, by suggesting that receiving the 6,000 rouble allowance was the only reason he carried on writing to her.

'Do you really believe me capable,' he replied, 'of remembering you only while I was using your money ? Could I really even for one moment forget what you have done for me, and how much I am indebted to you? I can say without exaggeration that you saved me, and that I should probably have gone out of my mind and perished if you had not come to my aid...'

He continued with outpourings of continued devotion, now to be free of any financial taint. Later, with Pachulski the only channel of communication, he expressed his hurt pride and the sense of betrayal. Both were strong but, from letters to Jurgenson, where he questions whether the whole story of money trouble was true, one suspects that there was a tinge of guilt too in Tchaikovsky's reaction. Nadezhda had loved him at a distance with a passion he had never been able to reciprocate, which was why he was so insistent that they should never meet. Her money had allowed him to live in a way it would have taken him another decade to achieve on his own. Yet all he had been able to offer her in return were letters of gossip, family intrigue, good prose and petulant artistry mixed with musical idealism. Their real love affairs, his sex life in the cafés of Paris and the palaces of Rome, and the affair which had produced her illegitimate daughter, Milochka, and caused her husband to die of heart failure – true intimacy – had always been hidden from each other. For two such complicated and emotional people it is less amazing that their relationship broke down as they grew older than that it lasted as long as it did.

Despite his propensity for emotional turmoil Tchaikovsky was professionally more resilient than even he gave himself credit for. The rupture with Nadezhda von Meck did not prevent him from continuing to sketch *The Voyevoda*, nor to leave Tblisi in triumph after conducting a full evening of his own music to tumultuous acclaim. On 3 November he crossed the Georgian mountains to visit Ippolit at Taganrog and then

The centre of Kiev with its Opera House, where *The Queen of Spades* was at first more warmly received than in St. Petersburg.

journeyed home to Frolovskoye for a fortnight before he was needed for rehearsals of *The Queen of Spades* in St Petersburg.

On the surface the premiere on 19 December 1890 was an immense public success with the audience heaping Tchaikovsky with compliments, ovations and wreaths. It soon became clear, though, that the enthusiasm was more for the composer himself than for the opera. The critics' reviews ranged from the coldly analytical to the sternly dismissive, comparing *The Queen of Spades* unfavourably with *Onegin* (which was fair) and *The Sorceress* (which was not). The gloom of reading these was partially alleviated by the much warmer reaction it received in Kiev on 31 December. There the company, controlled by its artists and not by imperial management, performed it with immediate sympathy. The reaction of the public was even more generous than it had been in Tbilisi and it was enough to make the Tchaikovsky brothers consider another collaboration later in the year, for the Imperial theatres had asked for both another opera and a ballet, *King Rene's Daughter* (a one-act play by Henrik Hertz) and a Petipa scenario based on E.T.A. Hoffmann's *The Nutcracker and the Mouse King*.

Once home again Tchaikovsky (after a quick visit to Kamenka, where he found Sasha in better form than usual) had to fulfil a commission that had been hanging over him for months and which he could barely summon the interest to begin: incidental music for *Hamlet*, starring Lucien Guitry in St Petersburg. He had agreed over two years earlier but in the meantime had treated the subject fully and felt no urge to do anything more with it. However he met the deadline and though he grumbled, the music pleased the public and himself more than he expected when it was performed on 21 February 1891.

At much the same time Tchaikovsky suffered one of his periodic fits of believing that nobody appreciated his music when news reached him that no further performances of *The Queen of Spades* were to be given that season. He feared it was because the Tsar had lost interest in him and that full houses were no longer enough. He therefore offered to withdraw from the two new commissions. The real reason – that the heroine, Medea Figner, was pregnant and her husband Nicholai refused to sing the hero's role with anyone else – was kept from him but, after making reassuring noises about continuing favour at court, Vsevolozshky gave the composer as accurate a character assessment as he was ever likely to receive:

'You have a strange and unhappy character, dear Pyotr Ilyich! You have a desire to torment and torture yourself with empty apparitions. Everyone knows your worth. To be precise, you are a Russian talent – real not hollow – therefore you do not possess over-confidence but excessive modesty.'

With his ego soothed, in March 1891 Tchaikovsky composed himself to start work on *The Nutcracker*. Only a week or so of work was possible, though. He had agreed, for a fee of $2,500 which was not to be ignored now that the von Meck allowance was ended, to conduct in the opening concert series at Carnegie Hall in New York. On the way he had arranged to spend two weeks with Modest enjoying themselves in Paris before his one engagement at the Châtelet, a complete programme devoted to his music with Sapelnikov in the *Second Piano Concerto* as the centrepiece. A week later a chance look at a Russian newspaper gave him the dreadful news that Sasha, on whom he had depended for so much of his life, had died. It was an appalling shock (which Modest had deliberately kept from him in case it made him turn back from his tour) but he rallied and on 18 March took ship from Le Havre.

The *New York Herald's* review of the inaugural concert in Carnegie Hall. *The Marche Slave* was 'a splendid greeting'.

The voyage lasted a week and it was far from comfortable. In that time they encountered the full force of a mid-Atlantic gale, fog off Newfoundland and the tail end of an East Coast hurricane. He was promptly engulfed in all the razzmatazz that a New York celebrity welcome could offer – a more comfortable hotel than he had ever found in Europe, mountains of flowers and newspapers overflowing with excitement about his visit. American fame had nothing reserved about it. His music was as well known as in Russia. He was fêted by the cream of New York artistic society, among them the philanthropist Andrew Carnegie and the 29-year-old conductor Walter Damrosch, whose New York Symphony Society Orchestra was to be the vehicle for the concerts (it was founded by his father Leopold and merged with the older but more sedate Philharmonic in

1928). The only thing that did not agree with him in the endless round of sumptuous luncheons and dinners that followed was American food, which he found 'unusually revolting'. At the hall's first concert on 5 May 1891, Tchaikovsky only conducted his *Coronation March*, Damrosch taking the lion's share with the Berlioz *Te Deum*. But there was a more substantial contribution two days later on his birthday when he conducted the *Third Suite*. The Tchaikovsky of ten years before would have been staggered to find himself hailed by the New York critics as one of the greatest of composer-conductors and among the most inspirational wielders of the baton the city had seen. The greatest success of all was the performance of the First Piano Concerto on 9 May, with Lizst's pupil Adele aus der Ohe as soloist.

Exhausted, he spent two days blissfully on his own at Niagara Falls and crossed into Canada. Then the business of the tour continued. The concerto was repeated in Baltimore and Philadelphia and the Russian Embassy threw an official party for him in Washington. On 20 May he embarked on the new German liner *Fürst Bismarck*, bound for Southampton and Cuxhaven, and he reached St Petersburg on 1 June 1891.

The torments of life without trees at Frolovskoye meant that he had no wish to live there anymore and he had made sure of booking a house at Maidanovo once again. It was in familiar surroundings, then, that he completed the preliminary work on *The Nutcracker*. Most of the First Act had been written before he left on his travels and, though it may have been augmented in France, the weather, the impact of Sasha's death and the unrelenting pace of the American schedule meant that nothing had been composed in May. Tchaikovsky made up for it with one of his bursts of creative energy, finishing *The Nutcracker* on 6 July and a fortnight later beginning the operatic part of the double bill, the title of which was changed to *Iolanta*. He was unhappy with the subject matter of the ballet, which he rightly thought was too frivolous for its length, and with Modest's weak libretto for *Iolanta*, which was even less satisfactory than that for *The Queen of Spades*. Nonetheless Tchaikovsky persevered and *Iolanta* was finished in September.

He was then faced with a mammoth task of orchestration, for *The Voyevoda* had to be finished as well, ready for its premiere on 18 November two nights after *The Queen of Spades* had been introduced to Moscow. Tchaikovsky took an instant dislike to the new tone poem and destroyed the score the next day. He would have torn up the orchestral parts too had Alexander Siloti not realised what was about to happen and confiscated

Carnegie Hall, New York
in its pomp.

CARNEGIE HALL

Copyright 1929 by ALFRED SCOTT. Publisher. 156 Fifth Ave., New York, N. Y.

them against the composer's orders. In truth they were both right. *The Voyevoda* is not good enough to be mature Tchaikovsky but neither is it bad enough music to be destroyed. It is an important document of his last years.

In 1892 Tchaikovsky's creative life slowed noticeably. Although he now looked ten years older than he was – as newspapers around the world kept reminding him – this was hardly because his powers were drying up, though periodically he wrote as much to Bob and Modest, usually when he had just finished a work and was not yet ready to begin another. Rather the business of being a famous composer was crowding him. His music was being gathered in large editions and the scores of new works were appearing in print much faster than before. This required an immense amount of proofreading, about which Tchaikovsky was something of a perfectionist, and the task was made even more wearing by his tendency to insist on last-minute alterations. Conducting had to be undertaken to underpin his finances, for though he lived as quietly as he could, he was immensely generous to others, whether they be Modest, promising students or distant relatives. All this cut into the speed with which he could orchestrate *Iolanta* and *The Nutcracker*.

At the beginning of 1892 he spent the Russian Christmas at Kamenka (sadly calm without the immediate family, Sasha, or her two dead daughters) after directing two concerts in Kiev. From there he went to Warsaw for more concerts and then to Hamburg to give *Onegin* in German. The one rehearsal allotted to him was not encouraging, however, and he was relieved to be able to hand over to a more experienced conductor whom he was coming to admire greatly, Gustav Mahler. By 21 January 1892 he was in Paris, intending to spend two weeks there before giving concerts in The Hague and Amsterdam (at the new and acoustically wonderful Concertgebouw). However for once Paris felt foreign and unamusing and while he did manage to revise *Souvenir de Florence*, winter depression got the better of him and he returned to St Petersburg early, having cancelled his appearances in the Netherlands.

In Maidanovo once again he was faced with a problem. Having destroyed *The Voyevoda* he had nothing new to perform at the RMS on 19 March. Making the best of a necessity he assembled a Suite from the unperformed *Nutcracker* music. This proved to be an inspired move for it not only proved instantly popular, it paved the way for the acceptance of the full ballet later in the year. *The Nutcracker Suite* was established and published as a separate work even before its parent was premiered. In April there was more solemn duty in St Petersburg when a Requiem Mass was celebrated in Sasha's memory.

That month was notable for an excursion which was unique in Tchaikovsky's experience: his appearance as an opera conductor of work other than his own. The co-operative company which had made such a success of *Onegin* in Kiev were touring to Moscow and Tchaikovsky, waiving his fee, agreed to help them attract an audience by conducting *Onegin* but also Rubinstein's *The Demon* (a staple of Moscow repertoire at the time) and Gounod's *Faust*. In late May he was free to return to the country but he had decided he needed a place of his own, especially since Alyosha had married again and was now a father. Maidanovo was becoming too much of a resort but

The programme for the production of *Evgeny Onegin* on 19 January 1892 in the Hamburg City Theatre. The conductor was 'Capellmeister Mahler'.

Stadt - Theater.
(Direction: B. Pollini).

Herr Hofrath **P. v. Tschaïkowsky**, der nach Hamburg gereist war, um die Erst-aufführung seiner Oper „**Eugen Onégin**" persönlich zu leiten, fühlt sich etwas unpäßlich und hat daher die Leitung der Vorstellung Herrn Capellmeister **Mahler** übertragen, wird derselben aber beiwohnen.

Hamburg, den 19. Januar 1892.

Die Direction.

Tchaikovsky liked the vicinity of Klin and he had settled on a villa on the edge of the town with a good size garden. It was to be his last home and is now the Tchaikovsky museum. There he wanted to resume his usual routine of writing a big work in time for the winter but the drudgery of mundane work on the *Iolanta* and *Nutcracker* scores, parts and proofs made concentration hard to achieve. Nonetheless during the summer months he did make headway with music for a new symphony. Normally he would be certain of his themes and sketch such a work within a month or so. The plan was there but real inspiration eluded him. It seemed as though after the creative spurt of the previous five years he was doomed to another hiatus like that which he suffered in the early 1880s. As it was he tackled two movements, then headed to France with Bob, a trip which was spoilt for them by the arrival of Anatoly's wife who seems to have made the constant mistake of falling for homosexual men adored by her brother-in-law and finding her heterosexual husband too dull.

There was another month away in September. This time he was due to conduct in Vienna but when he arrived he found the venue was a café and he left in disgust, instead spending two weeks at a Tyrolean castle belonging to Sapelnikov's lover, Sophie Menter. From there he went to Prague for the production of *The Queen of Spades*, the opera's most triumphant yet and far more warm in its reception than it had achieved in

Russia. It was not until November 1892 that the sketch of a symphony was ready and when, a month later, he came to begin the orchestration, he was profoundly dissatisfied with it. For the second time in a little over a year he found himself throwing out a major work. Perhaps this was accurate self-criticism or perhaps it was a reaction to the relative failure on 18 December of *Iolanta*, performed in a double bill with *The Nutcracker*. The opera was a hit with the audience, as it was when Mahler conducted it in Hamburg a fortnight later, but the press was scathing and professional opinion was that it was his weakest opera for a decade. On the evening, ironically, it was the ballet critics who liked *Iolanta* and the music critics who liked *The Nutcracker*: not a happy division.

Gustav Mahler, as fine an interpreter of his contemporaries' music as he was of his own.

January 1893 saw another round of travelling across Europe, initially from Berlin to Basel and then to Montbeliard, only 50 kilometres away. There he spent two days with his old nanny, Fanny Durbach, not in reality that much older than himself – she was only 70. It was an emotional meeting, prepared by letters over many months, and in retrospect, there was a poetic symmetry in returning to Fanny at the start of his last year. Once the correspondence started, after a gap of 37 years, it continued until the end. Just as he had as a boy, Tchaikovsky found his governess a rock of good sense and reassurance and she found her prize pupil just as tender and vulnerable as ever.

During the rest of January he marked time in Paris, becoming increasingly bored with his own company, and gave a charity concert in Brussels before heading for Odessa, where he was greeted by a throng at the station including Sapelnikov and Sophie Menter (one of whose works, which Tchaikovsky had orchestrated for her, was on the programme). He had come to conduct *The Queen of Spades*, three full concerts and token works in two others. Even by Tchaikovsky's increasingly exalted standards his reception in Ukraine's second city was astonishing. Entire works had to be repeated, individual movements received four encores, the orchestra members each queued to kiss his hands in turn. For posterity the most important accolade was the portrait painted by Nicholai Kuznetsov from sketches in rehearsals of the opera and in formal sittings in the theatre foyer. Kuznetsov finished the painting while the composer was in the city and Tchaikovsky was delighted by what was the only portrait (rather than photograph) for which he ever sat. It shows a distinguished and serious artist in late middle age, not the gaunt and harrowed figure of the late photographs. It is how Tchaikovsky wanted us to remember him. The adulation in Odessa contrasted with the relative indifference he suspected in Moscow, St Petersburg and Paris.

These contrasts – and perhaps the review of his life that he had undertaken in his two days with Fanny Durbach – were behind his determination to try again at writing another symphony when he returned home to Klin in February. He had tried to capture the essence of his life in the earlier attempt but had felt the material was seriously inadequate to the task. All his symphonies over the years had carried the same seed – a subjective programme of broad categories: love, fate, death, hope and disappointment. Now he wanted to put them all together in a complex structure that reflected the strength of his emotions, leavened by the triumphs and joys as well as weighted by the miseries. Like Elgar's *Enigma Variations* seven years later, the intention was to give the audience a riddle as to the precise meaning of the episodes. He wrote to Bob Davidov that it was to be called simply *Programme Symphony*, that it was to be thoroughly subjective and that, thinking it through on his train journeys, he had wept bitterly. Since Tchaikovsky was a great weeper and often cried as he wrapped himself in the emotional pathos of the scene he was composing, one should not see this as particularly out of the ordinary, less still some sort of premonition. Indeed it was the opposite; proof to Tchaikovsky that he still had really strong ideas left and was not creatively bankrupt after two years of major works which he realised were not in the same class as those of the late 1880s. Nor was the flow of inspiration confined to the new symphony. During the early spring of 1893 he also wrote the *Eighteen Piano Pieces*, Op. 72 (partly derived from material in the discarded symphony and each dedicated to a different friend), and the *Six Songs, Op.73*, neither of which suggests that everything he was composing then was tinged by any sense of desperation or fatalism, anymore than could be traced in any number of his works.

Nor was Tchaikovsky writing in deep seclusion. He arrived in Klin on 15 February and began work the next morning. A week later he reported to Bob that he had outlined the first movement in less than four days, that half the third movement was 'done' and that the shape of the rest was clear, including the fact that it was to end with a long adagio rather than the usual bangs and crashes. Then he went to Moscow to conduct at the RMS for the first time since 1890 (*Hamlet, The Nutcracker Suite* and the *Concert Fantasia*). From there he went to stay with Anatoly, whose postings had taken him from Tblisi via Tallinn to Nizhny-Novgorod. Only in between visits to St Petersburg

191

The piano room in Tchaikovsky's house at Klin, his last home.

and more conducting in Moscow and, in Ukraine again, Kharkov (where he was carried from the hall to the post-concert banquet by students) was he able to snatch time for the symphony. Yet despite this he was able to finish the sketches on 5 April and on the same day jot down a march for an infantry regiment of which his cousin Andrei was Commander. Then, after writing a piano piece a day for nearly three weeks, the six songs, visiting Anatoly again and hearing Rachmaninov's first important works, he left Klin for Cambridge.

He was not keen to cross to England again for the country had always depressed him and for once his longing for home had the good excuse that the symphony still needed to be orchestrated. Nonetheless he had promised Charles Stanford that he would attend Cambridge University Musical Society's Golden Jubilee celebrations, for only those there in person were to be granted honorary doctorates. More to the point it also gave him the chance to conduct a symphony in London, as he had promised the Philharmonic Society he would.

As usual he stayed at the Hotel Dieudonné and on 1 June shared the bill at St. James's Hall with Saint-Saëns and the Scottish composer, Alexander Mackenzie, whose account gives an engaging portrait of Tchaikovsky, though it has a tinge of inaccurate hindsight:

The Scottish Composer and Principal of London's Royal Academy of Music, Sir Alexander Campbell Mackenzie.

'When the famous Peter Ilitsch (sic) came to conduct his Fourth Symphony in '93 he seemed already a spent man, nor did he live very long after his visit; the weak voice, intense nervousness, and exhaustion after rehearsal, plainly indicated failing health. His

192

unaffected modesty, kindly manner and real gratitude for any trifling service rendered, all contributed to the favourable impression made by a loveable man. Truth to tell, Tchaikovsky possessed no gifts as a conductor, and knew it; nevertheless, thanks to the assistance of an attentive and sympathetic orchestra, No. IV scored a complete success. I fear to have unwittingly provided an uncomfortable hour for him when, honouring the Royal Academy of Music by a quite unexpected visit at a time when I happened to be exceptionally busy, I placed a baton in his hand and called upon a student to play his B flat minor concerto at an orchestral practice. The Philharmonic directors invited him to dinner at the St Stephen's Club, after which he and I started on a long ramble through the streets until past one o'clock in the morning. I then learned that he was neither a perfect Wagnerite nor a devout worshipper at the shrine of Brahms and gathered that his reception in Vienna had not been a pleasant one... He stated to me that the fight for recognition had been a hard one everywhere – but in England. Without showing discontent, or bitterness, the amiable Russian appeared melancholy and lonely; devoid of self-assertion and giving no sign of the passion and force revealed in his music.'

The conferment of the doctorate on 13 June, with all its peculiar ceremony which Tchaikovsky bore with good humour, was preceded by a concert the night before. Stanford's account is a little crusty but lucid:

'Saint-Saëns was chosen for France, Max Bruch for Germany, Tchaikovsky (then far less known in England than since his death) for Russia, Boito for Italy and Grieg for the North. They all accepted and came, with the exception of Grieg, who had, through illness, to postpone his visit to the following year. The programme contained one specimen of each composer, chosen by himself. Saint-Saëns played the solo part in *Africa*, Bruch conducted the scene of the Phoenicians from *Odysseus*, Boito the prologue to *Mefistofele*, Tchaikovsky the symphonic poem *Francesca da Rimini* which, as he wrote to me, he considered to be his best work in that style. Grieg was represented in absentia by *Peer Gynt*. The functions passed off without any hitches or difficulties. Whatever friction there might be between the composers' respective foreign offices, there was in Cambridge an entente cordiale which embraced the whole of Europe.'

Stanford adds two details which are fascinating. One is the suggestion that Tchaikovsky might have had Jewish blood because his name meant 'son of Jacob'. If so it would be ironic, for one of his few truly unattractive traits was lifelong general

Charles Villiers Stanford (1852-1924), as seen by Spy for *Vanity Fair.*

Nicholai Kuznetsov's (1850-1930) portrait of Tchaikovsky, painted in the theatre foyer in Odessa in 1893. Somehow it comes closer to its subject than any of the photographs.

anti-Semitism (though it does not seem to have been held against his Jewish professional friends). The other was a report.

'A very curious conversation took place in the train to Cambridge between him and a musical friend of mine. He told my friend of his having written the Pathetic (sic) Symphony (which had not yet been performed); that it originally was designed in three movements, but that after he had finished the third, something compelled him to add a tragic slow movement at the end; and that he added perhaps it was prophetic.'

From England Tchaikovsky claimed to be desperate to get home but in fact dawdled for the rest of the month, spending nearly a week in Paris and another at Menter and Sapelnikov's castle. In Russia he first went to see Kolya Konradi at

194

Grankino, really to spend time with Bob. There he started to work at last, although not on the symphony. Instead he fashioned what remained of its predecessor into a *Third Piano Concerto*, which left him two major works to orchestrate before the autumn concert season. Meanwhile old friends were dying: Karl Albrecht, both Shilovsky brothers and Apukhtin, all bad blows within weeks of each other. Yet Tchaikovsky seems to have borne the grief with unwonted fortitude. It seems his pleasure at being with Bob and his group, together with a real sense of artistic achievement during the year, was keeping depression – though not occasional melancholy as the composer in London had observed – at bay.

Ten days were spent with his brother Nicholai and he was

The house at Klin.

home in Klin at the end of July. He was thoroughly restless, even after months of travelling. He wanted to be with Bob, he agreed to go back to London the following May to conduct the *Sixth Symphony*, he was going to write another opera, probably on a George Eliot story, and to revise his unsatisfactory earlier efforts, *The Oprichnik* and *The Maid of Orleans*. However, for most of August he stayed put and concentrated on orchestrating the symphony.

At the beginning of September he spent a few days in St Petersburg and then a week in Hamburg supervising *Iolanta*. The latter half of the month he spent with Anatoly's family in the country, as he would have done in past years at Kamenka. But on the Ukrainian estate Lev had remarried, and without Sasha and the children, especially Bob, there was nothing to draw Tchaikovsky there anymore. For the first week in October he was in Moscow, watching Modest's boring new play and seeing Taneyev and Rachmaninov. On 7th he returned to Klin and two days later began to orchestrate the *Third Piano Concerto*. Only the first movement was ready by the time he returned to Moscow on 19th but he carried the work with him to show Taneyev. After two days he left for St Petersburg, the line taking him past his present home at Klin and his former ones at Maidanovo and Frolovskoye. The *Sixth Symphony* was to be given its premiere on 28th, along with the *First Piano Concerto*, in which Adele aus der Ohe was to repeat her interpretation of the American tour the year before. Tchaikovsky was right about the originality of the new symphony. Rehearsals were difficult, for the orchestra found it far harder to master than they usually did with his music and the premiere was greeted with baffled respect rather than rapture by the audience, no doubt disconcerted by the way the symphony fades away, rather than moving to a triumphant close. The next morning, as he prepared the score for despatch to Jurgenson, Tchaikovsky wondered what to call it. *Programme Symphony* no longer seemed enough. *Tragic Symphony* was too glib for a work of so many moods. It was Modest who suggested *Pathetique* and his brother accepted the idea as a solution, though in the light of what followed, one wonders whether his endorsement was quite as enthusiastic as Modest suggests. Within a week Tchaikovsky was dead.

How he died has been the subject of more disinformation, speculation, detective work and sheer fiction than has been the case for any composer other than Mozart (who actually died of long-standing kidney disease). There are two schools of argument: the official version, narrated by Modest and the Bertenson brothers, the Tsar's physicians who attended – that Tchaikovsky died of kidney failure after contracting cholera from drinking a glass of unboiled water – and the unofficial version circulating in Russia and, since 1979, in the rest of the world: variations on the theme that Tchaikovsky committed suicide after it became clear that he was about to be denounced to the Tsar for illegal homosexual activity with the nephew of Count Stenbok-Fermor and that he was compelled to do so on 31 October by a 'court' of eight old boys of the School of Jurisprudence, led by Nicholai Jacobi, Senior Procurator to the Senate.

The undisputed facts are that on 1 November Tchaikovsky had dinner with Vera Butakova, Lev Davidov's sister who had so loved him in their twenties. He then went to the Alexandrinsky Theatre to see a play by Ostrovsky. After the theatre he joined

A page from the manuscript of the Sixth Symphony.

a party of relatives and friends, including Glazunov and (later) Modest, at Leiner's restaurant where he ate macaroni and drank wine and mineral water (though his nephew Yuri said that the water he drank there was plain and unboiled). During the night he began to feel unwell and the next morning complained that he had a stomach upset. He went to see Napravnik but never arrived, turning back because he felt too ill. No doctor was called because he often suffered from a nervous stomach and it was assumed it was a reaction either to the food of the previous day or exhaustion after the premiere of the *Pathetique*. Modest says that it was then, at lunch, that he drank the famous unboiled water. If that was the case (and if Tchaikovsky did die of cholera) then it was certainly not the culprit. He was feeling ill already and cholera takes many more hours to incubate. On the other hand, if Yuri was right and the water was taken the night before at Leiner's, it could have been the culprit. By eight that evening (2 November) he was seriously ill with diarrhoea and nausea and the doctor was called. Over the following days three doctors attended. Cholera was diagnosed and its stages came and went. Tchaikovsky seemed to rally, just as his mother had done. Then on Sunday uraemia set in and just after three on the morning of Monday 6 November he died. With him were Nicholai and Modest, Bob Davidov, the servants Alyosha and Nazar, and Tchaikovsky's cousins Konstantin and Alexander Littke.

About all that can be said with certainty is that Tchaikovsky died at the age of 53 after a short illness surrounded by friends and family. His nephew Bob was made his heir. His last work, the *Third Piano Concerto*, was performed as a one movement piece in 1895 and a year later his pupil, friend and the only person he implicitly trusted to criticise his music, Sergei Taneyev, orchestrated the final two movements. Sadly the finished work, no less Tchaikovsky's than Mozart's *Requiem* is Mozart's rather than Süssmayer's, is rarely heard intact. On 18 November Napravnik conducted a second performance of the *Pathetique*. This time everyone understood what a quiet ending could mean.

There has to be a word about the rival theories of suicide and cholera stemming from incautious drinking of infected water, however. There is no doubt that the stories told by Modest and the doctors are inconsistent with each other. Tchaikovsky cannot have contracted cholera at lunchtime and been diagnosed as a classic case at 8 pm. The standard treatment given to cholera patients was a hot bath, given in the hope of maintaining circulation. Tchaikovsky had been at home when his mother had been treated in this way just before her death and he did not want to die the same way, according to Modest. Consequently the bath was not given until late in the proceedings, when the infectious stage of the cholera had passed and kidney failure was the most dangerous risk. Tchaikovsky emerged weaker than ever. The doctors were lambasted in the press for not administering this treatment earlier (not that it would have done much good). As to when the disease was contracted; given that he was feeling ill during the night of 1 November, it is more likely that he was infected that morning or sometime in the evening of 31 October.

The suicide theory suggests that a 'court of honour' took place earlier that day at which Tchaikovsky was instructed to kill himself, otherwise a letter of complaint and exposure would be written to the Tsar. For a moment let us accept that this was true. Between writing a letter to Willem Kes, the founding conductor of Amsterdam's Concertgebouw

Tchaikovsky with his nephew
and heir, Bob Davidov,
pictured in 1892.

Orchestra, in the morning, walking with Alexander Littke and
attending a performance of Rubinstein's opera *The Maccabees* in
the evening there would have been time for such a court to
convene. In which case there could be a grain of truth in the
glass of water story but it would have been drunk at least twelve
hours earlier than Modest suggested. Tchaikovsky had once
before tried suicide, during the disaster of his marriage. He
had tried then to find a way to shift the responsibility from
himself to nature by trying to catch his death in the Neva. If he
had to kill himself it is quite likely that he would have left it to
fate to decide whether he caught cholera and chosen a method
which was both deliberate and innocent and which was
common in St Petersburg; the same death that had taken away
his mother nearly 40 years before.

This assumes, however, that any group of acquaintances, none of them close to him, could have compelled Tchaikovsky to behave in such a way at a moment when he was Russia's most adored artist and the rest of the world was queuing up to sing his praises. If there had been threat of disgrace in Russia, surely he would just have taken a train to Paris where he could enjoy his sexual preferences as he liked with virtually no public comment? There is an assumption, too, that sending a letter to the Tsar would have created a homophobic reaction that would have destroyed Tchaikovsky's reputation and that of the School of Jurisprudence. This is highly unlikely. The School of Jurisprudence had been as famous as many other boys' schools for its homosexual graduates, Apukhtin and Prince Meshchersky among them. Tchaikovsky was at the centre of a group of known homosexual artists and aristocrats, including junior members of the Royal Family. Telling the Tsar that would have been no news at court. Alexander III might have had a cross word but there would have been no permanent disgrace. While homosexual activity was illegal, proving a complaint entailed such a convoluted police process that it was almost never attempted. Russia was not England. The Russian Orthodox Church did not meddle with people's sex lives as the Roman Catholic and Protestant churches love to do. Tchaikovsky was not in the same danger as Oscar Wilde. The suicide theory is possible but the more one inspects it the more pointless it becomes. It is much more likely that Tchaikovsky, like hundreds of others that autumn, contracted cholera and succumbed, the only inaccuracy being in Modest's amateur attempt at explaining how and when the infection took place. Cholera was rife in the city. That is why visitors to the dying man were only allowed in after the most infectious stage had passed and why the flat was disinfected, Tchaikovsky's face being wiped with disinfectant as friends lined up to pay their affectionate respects as he lay in his open coffin and the mass for the dead was read.

60,000 applied for tickets to his funeral in St Kazan's Cathedral, organized as the great theatrical event it undoubtedly was by the directorate of the Imperial Theatres. Only 8,000 could be let in. In a gesture accorded previously only to Pushkin as a Russian Artist the Tsar paid for the ceremony. Crowds lined the streets as the coffin was carried to the Cathedral and again as it was taken to the Alexander Nevsky cemetery. For Tchaikovsky perhaps the greatest honour he would have felt would not have been the State Funeral, unprecedented for a commoner as it was, but that he was buried near Glinka.

At the end there can have been no question that the people of Russia regarded him as their greatest artist. He was venerated in a way impossible for modern society, used to artists being a minor part of the entertainment business, to understand. Only ten months before he had written to Anatoly, 'today is the fourth day that the whole of the Petersburg press is occupied in attacking my latest progenies – one newspaper after another. But I am completely indifferent to it all, being certain that my day will come.'

Further Reading

Abraham, Gerald. *Studies in Russian Music* (London, 1935).
  Tchaikovsky (London, 1944)
  Slavonic and Romantic Music (London, 1968)

Brown, David. *Tchaikovsky Remembered* (London, 1993)
  Tchaikovsky - The Early Years (London, 1978)
     - The Crisis Years (London, 1982)
     - The Years of Wandering (London, 1986)
     - The Final Years (London, 1991)

Calvocoressi, M.D., and Abraham, Gerald
  Masters of Russian Music (New York, 1944)

Mackenzie, Sir Alexander Campbell. *A Musician's Narrative*
  (London, 1927)

Montagu-Nathan, M. *A History of Russian Music* (London, 1914)

Mundy, Simon. *Alexander Glazunov* (London, 1987)

Norris, Gerald. *Stanford, The Cambridge Jubilee and Tchaikovsky*
  (Newton Abbott, 1980)

Poznansky, Alexander. *Tchaikovsky, The Quest for the Inner Man*
  (New York, 1991)

Rimsky-Korsakov, Nicholai (trans. Judah A. Joffe)
  My Musical Life (New York, 1942)

Ronald, Sir Landon. *Tschaikowsky* (London, 1912)

Stanford, Sir Charles Villiers. *Pages from an Unwritten Diary*
  (London, 1914)

Stasov, Vladimir (trans. F. Jonas). *Selected Essays on Music*
(London 1968)

Swan, Alfred J. *Russian Music* (London, 1973)

Tchaikovsky, Pyotr Ilyich (trans. Galina von Meck).
  Letters to His Family (New York, 1982)

Warrack, John. *Tchaikovsky* (London, 1973)

Index